Stephan Ross is an ordained elder in the Oregon-Idaho Conference of the United Methodist Church. Ordained in 1982, he served from then until 2010 in a variety of local churches in Oregon and Idaho. He has served congregations, sometimes two at a time, ranging from eighteen to 250 in weekly worship attendance. He has served rural, very small town and county seat churches. Of the six congregations Steve served, two of them experienced significant renewal of their vitality and numeric growth during his service as pastor. From 2010 to 2012 Steve served as a Superintendent in the Oregon Trail District, and from 2012 to 2017 as Director of the Vital Church Project for the Oregon-Idaho Conference. In that position Steve's focus was on establishing new faith communities for new people, revitalization of existing congregations, and leadership development for congregational excellence.

Contents

Prologue 5

Chapter One: It Begins with Mission 11

Chapter Two: Leadership Matters....................................37

Chapter Three: Principles of Effective Church Leadership 61

Chapter Four: Governance, Management and Ministry 81

Chapter Five: An Empowering Organization..................101

Chapter Six: Empowering Leaders 121

Chapter Seven: The Church Council 143

Chapter Eight: Staff...175

Chapter Nine: Ministry Teams 197

Appendix A: United Methodist Process for Adopting Simple
    Governance..209

Appendix B: Oregon-Idaho Model for Simple Governance
    Structure 210

Appendix C: Detailed Council Agenda Annual Cycle 215

Appendix D: Town Hall Meetings.................................226

Annotated Bibliography..230

Prologue

There's nothing sexy about this topic. Dealing with how leaders lead and what kind of structure best serves the church doesn't feel very spiritual to most people. For one thing, most of the issues relating to leadership and structure are true for all organizations, not just churches, so it doesn't seem very "spiritual."

It reminds me of how many people feel about law. In general, they don't want any. But when their neighbor has his stereo turned up at 2 AM they call a cop and expect something to be done about it. It's the same with administrative structures. We mostly find maintaining them a nuisance (and we consider the people who ask us to maintain them somewhat irritating). But when we need help, we almost always wonder why they don't do a better job for us.

There really is no "paradigm of leadership" which best serves all Christian communities for all time. Leadership is, and will always remain, an art.

About the only art I have personal experience in is building a wooden sailboat. Good wooden boats are both beautiful and functional. The art of building a wooden boat is about creating a form out of wood that is aligned with the forces of wind and water in a way that gracefully, safely and efficiently bears the boater across the water. It's amazing really, when it all comes together.

A truly great wooden boat builder (which I am not) brings something indefinable and un-teachable to the art. Nevertheless, boat builders must all learn the qualities and limitations of their materials. Some of the wood they use needs to be strong, some flexible, some rot-resistant. They need to use the right wood in the right place. They learn to use fasteners made of copper, bronze or stainless steel to prevent rust. They learn which oils, varnishes and paints will last. As a church leader the materials you must learn to appreciate include the people in your congregation, the people in your mission field, financial resources, and facilities.

When boat makers build, it is essential that they accept and align with the natural forces of wind and water that their boat will be dependent upon and subject to. Every detail of the boat must be consistent with these forces or it will fail to go where you want it to take you. Church leadership requires that we accept and align our work with the forces of Holy Spirit and human nature. In addition, there are all those forces out there in the culture around us that, whether we consider them friendly or not, must be considered and respected.

Finally, boat builders have to learn how to use the tools and skills of their craft - riveting with hammers and roving irons; shaping with planes, spoke shaves, mallets and chisels; lining and spiling with dividers and battens. The tools and skills of leadership include meeting agendas, relationships, recruiting, job descriptions, committees, coaching, communicating, trust, training and so on. This book help be more aware and intentional about both the medium and tools of leadership.

All organizational structures are compromises. Bigger organizations can generate more resources and command more attention in a vast and highly distracted culture with vast and intractable problems. On the other hand, smaller organizations tend to engender greater individual participation and responsibility, both of which are essential for really life-changing discipleship. Smaller organizations are nimble, but small groups also seem more prone to become ingrown. There are parts of Christ's mission that are simply beyond the capacity of small congregations and parts that big congregations fail in. Big and small organizations are not just different in size, but also in character. They bring different gifts to human experience. They require different kinds of structures in order to function well.

Size is not the only difference relevant to organizational structure. Different cultural groups bring different demands and expectations to their organizational practices. Different purposes require different shapes of organizational structure. This means that the appropriate organizational structure is going to depend on what your group wants to accomplish and what kinds of resources and people you are working with. Asking which organizational structure is best may be a bit like asking what kind of vehicle is best - it depends on whether you want to haul your child to school in town or a few tons of wheat across the state. It depends on what you can afford and what you know how to drive. It depends.

So, this book is not designed to give you a model of leadership and structure that can solve all problems faced by all churches. It is not a book on the proper (or biblical) way to structure every congregation or church. There is no such thing. This book will focus on leadership and organizational practices and structures that seem to work best in mainline Protestant congregations with about 50 to 500 people in worship. It is a book about how simple governance can help your struggling congregation accomplish its mission during the early decades of the 21st century.

While I hope that this book might be of use to many congregational leaders in a variety of denominations it is written by a United Methodist especially for the people of my tribe who love the faith their church has nurtured in them and who realize that their church is not reaching others as well as they hope. This book is for people who are determined to find a way to "pay forward" the indescribable gift and blessing of faith no matter what it takes.

What it takes in our situation is a solution that moves us forward and outward now. I doubt it will be very long before someone will be writing about the problems our solutions have created. It's a good thing God is good, patient with us, and has a sense of humor.

I hope this will be a book that helps you make sense of the medium and the tools of leadership and organization in a way that will help your church now. The art will be up to you, and God. I'm confident that you and God are up to the challenge.

Study Questions

Why are you interested in the organization and leadership of churches?

Recall a time when you found church leadership frustrating. What was the source of frustration?

Recall a rewarding experience of church leadership. What made that experience a positive one for you?

What do you hope a change in structure or leadership practice can do for your church?

Chapter One
It Begins with Mission

When I was a kid I used to read the magazine *Popular Mechanics*. Every issue contained several articles about how you could make all kinds of things yourself. I remember being fascinated by articles with titles like *A Boat You Can Build This Weekend*, *Patio Furniture You Can Make Yourself,* or even *Putting Together Your Own AM Radio Receiver*.

Of course, I never actually made my own patio furniture or radio receiver and I didn't build my own boat until 2008. Building something isn't simply a matter of know-how. Building something requires dedicating precious time, spending limited money, and mastering relevant skills. Getting something done is not just a matter of knowledge; it is also a matter of motivation. Until you are motivated, until you want to build that thing enough to NOT do something else instead, reading the articles in Popular Mechanics is just pastime, not preparation.

This book is about how to build and maintain a church organization that can allow your congregation to thrive. Building and maintaining such an organization will take time and money and require mastering some skills. It will require you to give some things up, but it will also require sacrifices from other people in your congregation. If anything is ever going to happen, you must begin with motivation. A vital church is a wonder to behold and to be part of, but church as pastime? Not so much. Motivation in a church comes from one thing, and one thing alone - mission.

You are going to see that word *mission* quite a lot as we work on leadership and structure. I use the word mission to mean the shared intention that provides the motivating force that must be present to transform a bunch of individuals into a real community of people. This transforming power is present only when a group of people has a shared intention – a mission.

The strangers who ride the bus together every day to and from work are not a community even though they spend a couple hours a day together, but these people may suddenly become a kind of community if the bus gets stuck in a snowdrift. If that occurs, they may all get off to lighten the load. Some of them may organize to scoop snow away from the wheels and others to push on the front end as the bus driver backs out. All this happens because they have discovered a shared intent and it motivates them to accomplish something together. This is why so many people express the amazing sense of community that neighbors find when there is a natural disaster. It has given them a shared intention, and that is what makes a bunch of people into a community.

The shared intent of a vital congregation is historically referred to as a mission. The word has been adopted, it seems, by every other organized community in the world. All kinds of groups now make a big deal of their "mission." When everyone is using the word mission to describe their shared intent we in the church (who own this word!) may get cynical about the word and concept. "Oh no. Not another mission statement process." But vital congregations are always driven by a compelling and clear sense of the mission that God has given them. A real mission is so much more than just a clever mission statement. And it is definitely not just a marketing tool. It is a uniting purpose that resides in the life of every person in the church. A church without a real mission is like a car without fuel. It's a doorstop, a lump, a useless hunk of stuff that just requires upkeep but produces no output.

A real mission - one that inspires the people touched by it to devote their time and money and mastery to it - is inspired. Literally. A real mission is an intention shared by all the people in the church. The mission of a vital church is an intention shared by all the people who claim, "This is my church," and who devote

> *A community is something real. It becomes a part of the identity of every person who actually belongs to the community. It changes the lives of the people in the community and of the people touched by the community.*

themselves to its success. But the mission of a vital church is not just about the shared intention of a bunch of people. A mission requires that another One share its intention - and that other One is God.

The mission of a vital congregation is the shared intention given by God to a group of disciples, revealed to them in Jesus Christ and empowered in them by the Holy Spirit. *"Unless the Lord builds the house, those who build it labor in vain."* (Psalm 127:1 NRSV) Often, when a congregation is suffering from a failure to thrive, the reason is the lack of a mission.

Before you begin to figure out how to lead, or how to organize your church, you will need to figure out the mission that God is calling you and your congregation to fulfill. Without the mission, all the rest is absurd, and you will create only exhaustion and frustration for yourself and your church.

Discerning the Mission

For the past two decades or so the whole matter of mission, vision, purpose, goals, strategies, tactics, and so on has become so ubiquitous and confusing that most of us glaze over before the conversation even begins. We immediately imagine a Saturday at a retreat center with plenty of flip charts and sticky notes. We have done it with our church, our service club, and the people at work. Every one of those produced a three-ring binder or a bumper sticker statement that was forgotten on a shelf within two months.

Please don't shut down yet. If I could create a whole new vocabulary for this work I would, but I'm terrible at inventing words. So, let me instead reclaim the words *mission, vision, and values* in this book by laying out what I mean when I use them. We need to have a shared vocabulary. Since I don't know what your vocabulary is, I'm stuck with sharing mine with you.

Defining "Mission"

By *mission* I mean the underlying, driving, purpose for the community. In The United Methodist Church we have the good fortune of having the mission identified by our denomination. The United Methodist Discipline says that the mission of The United Methodist Church is making disciples of Jesus Christ for the transformation of the world. This basic mission statement is a recasting of the teaching of our founder, John Wesley. He taught that the Christian life consists of personal (discipleship) and social (world-transforming) piety.

If you are a United Methodist, your congregation does not need to develop a mission statement. It has one that will do quite nicely. If you are not a United Methodist, you are welcome to use the one your denomination has created, to create one yourself, or to use

> *If someone were to ask you, "What do the people in your church do? Why do they exist?" you should immediately be able to answer, and so should everyone in your church.*

this one. (We do not claim any exclusive rights to making disciples or transforming the world). In creating a mission statement of your own, you will want to refer to Jesus for some guidance in what that mission should be. (That last part is ironic understatement, just in case you aren't catching the tone in my voice.) The best place to find that guidance is in the Gospels and The Acts.

Let's use that United Methodist mission statement as an example and look at what makes it a mission statement. A mission statement should express the underlying, unchanging, determinative purpose of a group of people that distinguishes it from other groups. Making disciples of Jesus Christ distinguishes us from a lot of other communities. That is not the mission of public schools, Microsoft, the Elks Lodge, or the synagogue down the street. But "making disciples of Jesus Christ" sounds like it could be part of the mission of all the

Baptists, Presbyterians, Congregationalists, Lutheran or any number of other churches that I know.

We United Methodists have that second clause, "for the transformation of the world," because we began as a movement of people who were already baptized members of the Church of England, but who wanted to experience more of the kingdom of God in our own lives and communities right now. So, from our very roots we have been people who wanted to put those two things together, personal holiness (discipleship) and social justice (world transformation).

There are lots of really good people we know who are trying to transform the world who aren't particularly interested in following Jesus, and quite a few we know who are trying to follow Jesus in their own lives but aren't particularly interested in changing the world. We want to be people who do both things at the same time.

Your mission should be something like that - a relatively brief description of the purpose of your church. If someone were to ask you, "What do the people in your church do? Why do they exist?" you should immediately be able to answer, and so should everyone in your church. For United Methodists the answer to the question, "Why does the United Methodist Church exist?" is, "To make disciples of Jesus Christ for the transformation of the world." That's a good answer for those of us in churches that are motivated by being part of that purpose.

That kind of an answer is also good for people outside of our community. "Oh," they might say, "Thanks. Not interested."

Think of the time we save them not having to hang out with us for a few months or years trying to figure out what we're really all about and whether it matters to them. Or, they might say, "Interesting, tell me more. What is a disciple? How are you transforming the world? And if I want to be one of you, how will I do that?" That's the trouble with (and the power of) really good mission statements. They either turn people away in disinterest, or they lead to more questions.

Defining "Vision"

Every congregation needs to come to terms with those follow-up questions. I would call the answers to the follow-up questions a vision. What does a disciple look like to us here and now? John Wesley said a lot of things about what Methodist disciples looked like in his day. They didn't wear any jewelry and dressed plainly. They didn't get drunk (though they did enjoy a fine ale). They visited people in prison and they tended to their neighbors who were sick. They went to their Anglican Church every Sunday for communion (at a time when Anglicans who were not Methodists went once a year). They attended their "class meeting" every Wednesday evening where they prayed, meditated upon scripture, and engaged in holy conversations.

How did they transform the world? They were pacifists. They endeavored to earn their living only in ways that did not harm others. They agitated for reform of the British prison system. They started schools for poor children. They opposed slavery in Britain and America. Not every individual Methodist fully accepted or lived out all these things, but if you didn't others

> *A vision answers the important questions around how your congregation embodies and fulfills the mission (which is not changing) in its*

assumed you should. These were some of the things Methodists were "known for."

A hundred years later, the specific practices and world-transforming efforts of Methodists had shifted a bit. Most of them refused to drink any kind of alcohol. They gathered for camp meetings every summer. They were still fighting against (or defending!) slavery in a divided church in America. They had mostly rejected pacifism. They didn't play cards or dance. They were transforming the world by starting colleges, hospitals, creating (along with others) the YMCA to give young men in industrial cities something productive to fill their time, and they were advocating for workers' rights and universal education.

A vision answers the important questions around how your congregation embodies and fulfills the mission (which is not changing) in its place and time (which is constantly changing). The vision is more of an ongoing conversation than a statement that fits on a bumper sticker. A vision is the result of a conversation that revolves around some driving questions that reside at the center of a vital congregational.

- **Who is your congregation helping to become disciples?** Who is God sending you to invite into discipleship? The answer to this question should be specific. It may be the people in a specific geography. It may be people of a specific culture or ethnicity or generation. It may be people of a certain circumstance (poor or single parents). Whoever it may be, it will be people God has actually entrusted to your congregation. You will be expected to love them. Who is your neighbor?

- **What is your rule of life for fulfilling the mission?** How do you act in order to accomplish the purpose God has given you? What should you do? How is your mission distilled into actions, values, practices and behaviors that will be evident to anyone who observes the way that you live? How do you pray, worship, serve, and speak? What do you need to learn and do to be a disciple here?

- **How are you transforming the world?** What is God calling you to accomplish in yourselves, your community and the world? What are the needs and assets in your community? Are you focused on hunger, homelessness, social justice, liberation, healing, comfort, creation, or some other aspect of the totally redeeming mission of Jesus to the world? What are your individual and collective skills? What are the resources at your disposal? Where are you located (or where are you going)? What do you care about and what are your passions?

Defining "Values"

Every community is held together by some core values that take priority. One of the grave mistakes that Christian congregations can make is to forget that the first value for every church must be to fulfill the mission of Jesus Christ in their place and time. Too often we put many other values higher than the mission. We value "peace in the family" or "our own comfort," or "the admiration of our neighbors" more than we value the mission. Such congregations do not thrive, because God created the church for mission – to be the Body of Christ.

Once the mission is firmly in first priority, however, different congregations will order their values in a variety of ways. Perhaps God has created so many congregations so that all the values God has created in the world can be embodied.

Your congregation will not be able to live a coherent and fruitful life if it is not clear about its priority values. These values will also provide some of the boundaries within which your people find their common ground. One persistent Methodist value has always been simplicity. What simplicity looks like changes with the cultural context, but we have never been fancy people. Another value we have always held high is usefulness. We like people who contribute to the value of their community. We value that more, for example, than being able to quote scripture chapter and verse. What are the priority values of your congregation?

Please understand; being clear about your core values does not imply that you don't affirm other values. Almost all human beings have a very similar long list of values. Most of these values aren't even unique to Christianity. We have a lot of common ground with all of humanity. As Jesus said, "even thieves love their friends." Your congregation must discern is the short list of eight or ten values that characterize the people who can find a challenging and affirming spiritual home in its community of practice and belief.

Discerning and Articulating your Mission, Vision and Values

How does this happen in a congregation? Where does clarity about mission, vision and values come from?

How to determine The Mission

The purpose of a mission statement is to provide the point of light on the horizon that guides your congregation forward. It will not be detailed enough to define all your actions. The mission should just be the focal point to which everyone in the congregation can look for direction.

If you're lucky, you have a mission statement already. Check to see if your church already has a mission statement that has been neglected. It may be that you only need to resurrect the one that is already there. If it is longer than one or two sentences, edit it down.

If your church does not have a mission statement it should be prepared by a small group of your highly committed, and highly respected disciple/leaders. They will share their core scriptures, talk about their highest aspirations for the church and share what they feel God is calling your church to accomplish for the realm of God. This should not be a church-wide process and should not require a bunch of meetings. If at all possible you should avoid having to "vote" on it.

When you get your mission statement done it should state your purpose. It should be short enough for everyone to recognize. It should be simple and memorable enough for many of your people to be able to recite from memory. Those are qualities that are usually best expressed by a single author who has worked with a small group on the ideas and then written the statement (for the community) all by herself.

Once your trusted leaders have hammered out what they think is a statement that captures the overall purpose of your church, roll it out to the congregation. Have a series of worship services on the parts of the mission statement. Talk about what it means and how it is already expressed in the life of your congregation. Include the mission statement on your website, in your weekly bulletin, in the footer or header of your emails, letterheads, newsletters and brochures. Touch on it regularly in your meetings. Ask how this thing we are planning to do helps us to fulfill our mission. If your mission statement raises the right questions, it's a good one.

How to discern The Vision

Once you have a mission statement you can begin to discern and articulate the vision of the congregation. A vision cannot be given to your congregation by anyone else. You can't find one somewhere else that "sounds pretty good so let's just use it." Where a mission statement could work for many congregations over a long period of time, this is not true of a vision. The purpose of the vision statement is to answer the core question, "How are we going to express the mission of our church right here in our time and place?" Let me use The United Methodist Mission statement as an example.

If our mission is to make disciples of Jesus Christ for the transformation of the world, then we need to know to <u>whom</u> we are sent to make disciples, <u>how</u> we help people become disciples, and <u>what</u> we are called to transform in the world. Whatever your mission statement is, you will need to discern what the incarnation of that mission will look like in your congregation.

A vision does not need to be a short memorable statement. It does need to sketch a memorable "picture." One church I know has a vision description that covers one whole side of a legal-size sheet of paper. It describes in some detail the kind of people they are trying to reach. It talks about the things that people in their church will be doing to bless the community. It describes the practices that help people in their church grow up in their discipleship. Nobody would ever think of memorizing it. But everyone has that picture of their future in their head. It forms the basis of the information that you can find on their website. It drives the kinds of brochures that they have created, and it helps them decide what sorts of ministries they put energy into. It even provides inspiration to new people who find a home with them and invent new ministries that help them grow into their vision. The vision provides the kind of clarity that helps your members make everyday choices that express the purpose of your congregation in their own lives.

How do you discern the vision? The process of visioning will involve many conversations and a variety of ways to access the passion, dreams and aspirations of the congregation. It also involves attention to the people outside your church who occupy your mission field.

A fruitful and powerful vision will emerge through attention to a number of different types of information from diverse sources and means of listening. As these streams of information flow together an increasingly useful picture of the vision of the congregation will begin to develop for those who are paying attention.

Who discerns the vision? Let's be clear that the vision originates in God who gives gifts, concerns and passion to the people in your congregation and who has placed your congregation where it is at this time. But the vision must be gathered, discerned, and articulated by people who are in a position to get this information together. So, let's talk about what some of those kinds of information are, and some ways you can gather them.

Who are we as a congregation?

What are our gifts and abilities?

- *What comes easy to your congregation?* Can they get a potluck together at the drop of a feather? Will they eagerly show up for a Bible study? Do they like speaker's forums on current issues? If you ask for someone to help an elderly lady clean her gutters do you need an arm wrestling match to determine who gets to do it? Is it reading groups, fund-raisers, mission trips, door-to-door campaigns or mother's nights out? The things that come easy reveal the natural giftedness of your congregation.

- *What does your congregation complain about and dream about?* Church leaders hate complaints, but sometimes they reveal concerns. What is on the other side of that complaint coin? When you ask people what their highest hopes are for the congregation, what are the common themes of their answers? What are people saying we need more of? These complaints and hopes help reveal the calling of your congregation.

> *A vision does not need to be a short memorable statement. It does need to sketch a memorable "picture."*

- *What are recurring themes from the oral history of your congregation?* Do they tell stories about the buildings they have built or the community programs they were running? What do people say was going on at the high points? (Why were those the good old days? Ask deeper questions about that.) What is the common narrative about how this congregation started or how it became what it is? These stories reveal the vision of your congregation.

- *What are the current assets and liabilities?* How old are we? How much time do our people have to give? What are our financial and facilities resources? Where are we located? What kinds of jobs are do our people have? What do they do for fun? These things reveal the assets (and challenges) of your congregation.

How do we collect this information?

- *Have a series of small group listening meetings.* Ask every person in turn to share: What is your family situation? What do you experience as the best thing about our church? What is the greatest challenge to our church right now? Describe your highest hopes for our church five years from now?

  Record on a simple form the basic answer you receive from every person. After collecting these from as many in the congregation as possible, have a group of leaders all read them and then discuss the major themes they see.

- *Have a small group of volunteers do 1-to-1 visits.* Each person on your 1-to-1 team agrees to interview five to seven people of their choosing from your congregation. The conversations last 30 – 45 minutes each and occur over a two to four-week period. The volunteers will begin the conversation with, "Tell me a little bit about you." From that point the volunteers will try to go deeper into whatever topic the person raises in the first question. The last movement of the conversation is to ask, "Is there any way in which your church does, or could, encourage you or help you to express (this thing that you care about so deeply)." After all the conversations have happened, your volunteer group gathers to discuss "what we learned about our church community" (not details from individuals!). The idea is to uncover common themes. What are the common hopes, concerns, values and passions of our people?

- *Have the congregation build a narrative timeline.* Place a long sheet of butcher paper on a suitable wall space. At one end put the date of the founding of this church with hash marks for decades or some other suitable time-frame across the middle of the sheet up to the current moment. Invite people to take a month or so to add sticky notes or to write on the timeline things from the life of the congregation (above the line) or in their lives or the community (below the line) that they think are "part of our story." Be sure to include both victories and crises.

- *Get the basic statistical and financial data for as many years as you can (at least ten and preferably twenty).* Have someone who is good with numbers and data prepare some charts for you showing the ebb and flow of attendance, membership, and so on during the years for which you have data.

- *Get a small vision group to spend some good focus time with the information gathered.* Make sure everyone in your vision team has time to read and digest the information gathered. Get together in a retreat setting for at least a day and a half and discuss your impressions. Who have we been at our best and worst? Where have we come from? What are our gifts and gaps? What are our dreams and hopes?

What is your mission field?

- *Who are the people in your community?* Determine the geography of your ministry area. This will depend on where you are. For congregations in large urban areas it

27

will depend on whether you are located at a freeway interchange or in an off-the-beaten-path neighborhood. If you are in a small or rural town, it may extend many miles into the country. It may go miles in one direction and stop two blocks away in the other direction because there is a river. It may be as simple as a zip code or a three-mile radius. Get a map and draw on it. Now, get good up-to-date demographic data on that region. Your denomination can probably help you with this.

- *What are the challenges and assets in your community?* What are the major institutions (schools, hospitals, religious groups, civic and service clubs, government agencies, etc.) in and reaching your mission area? What are the economic forces (major employers, major industries)? What are the physical and environmental qualities and characteristics of your mission area (parks, hot or cool summers, long snowy winters or mild, nearby mountains, rivers, lakes, or other outdoor attractions)? What are the recreational opportunities that characterize your mission field (organized sports, outdoors activities, book or card clubs, arts and culture)? What are the major problems in your community (drugs/alcohol, mental health, educational dysfunctions, ethnic or race strife, economic or environmental problems, healthcare access)?

How do we collect this information?

- *Demographic services:* MissionInsite and Perceptgroup are two companies that provide excellent demographic data for whatever mission area you need. They can include not just the normal demographic data, but also religious types, consumer types, activity preferences and other very useful information.

- *Civic Leader interviews:* Ask the police chief or sheriff, the school superintendent or principal, a hospital administrator or ER nurse or doctor, a county mental health worker or parole officer, the local newspaper publisher, and a small business owner what they see as the major assets and challenges for your community. Ask the high school student council president what he or she sees as the biggest challenge faced by young people.

- *Read the newspaper (online if you need to):* Have your team collect the most significant local news story each week for discussion when they gather.

- *Check your County website:* Most counties host websites that include data about the economic performance and demographic trends in the county. There are often other kinds of information that you can scan for interesting or useful bits of insight into your community.

- *Check with your local Chamber of Commerce, City Club or Downtown Association:* Many communities have some or all of these organizations (sometimes with slightly different names) and they are full of people who care about the community and are striving to make it a better place.

- *Get your small vision group to spend some good focus time with the information gathered.* Same thing as getting a picture of your congregation, only now you want a picture of your community. Be very careful not to fall into a common trap, which is the belief that you already know your community. Often what we think we know about our community is 20 or 30 years out of date. Or we are only aware of the part of it we are comfortable with and are astoundingly unaware the parts of our community we do not mingle in. Have each person share something he or she has learned and then build a picture together of your community that actually reflects the richness of its current reality.

Putting together the vision

Now that you have taken a deep and realistic look at your congregation and your community, your vision team should connect these two images through these significant questions:

- Which groups of people and/or problems in our community do we seem most concerned for as a congregation?

- Which groups of people in our community could most share in and contribute to the fulfillment of our highest dreams and hopes for our church?

- What abilities and assets that we possess in our congregation might best be used to engage in connection and relationship with these groups in our mission field?

- What needs and aspirations do these groups cherish that we might help them achieve? (Do NOT assume you can guess what these are. You are likely to assume they want to be more like you. You will need to learn this from them.)

- What groups of people in your mission field are already being well served by some other Christian church in your mission area? (Why would God want you to focus on them too?)

- DO NOT pay much attention to which is the largest demographic segment in your area.

- DO NOT assume that you must be focused on the neediest demographic in your neighborhood (nor should you assume you are not!).

- DO seek the affinities that exist between the people you are and the people you are being sent to.

Having discussed these questions in some depth, have your team begin to talk together about how you would describe yourselves and the groups of people you feel called to serve thriving together five years down the road.

- What do we look like together?

- What are we doing with one another to grow as disciples?

- What are we doing to bless one another and the community in Jesus name?

Talk about these things until, together, your team can talk about that vision as though they have time-traveled forward into it together and come back to tell the story.

Now, roll it out with the congregation. Yes, do a preaching series on "the church God is calling us to be." But also talk about it in the parking lot, in the social hour, at the committee meetings and the fellowship groups. Because you have done the listening well, when you begin to talk about who God is calling you all to become, your congregation will say, "Yes! That is who we are and who we want to be!" (If they don't, then listen to them some more and adjust until that happens.)

Discerning our Core Values

Don't worry. This is easier. Don't ask everyone what values your congregation places at highest priority. Everyone always answers the same – and the answer given is what we think **ought** to be our highest values. Your vision team should first look at some very objective data. How do we spend our money in this church? How do we use our facilities in this church? Who do we pay attention to and who gets ignored in this church? Who and what gets the pastors time? Which committees and teams actually function, and which can't seem to get off the ground? This hard data will give you some idea of the values that are <u>practiced</u>. Write down those practiced values.

Then, do a survey using a list of 20 value phrases that seem meaningful to your vision team. Use words like: tradition, relevant, biblically-based, young people, older people, new Christians, high commitment, community service, piety (holiness), diversity, orthodoxy, excellence, accepting. Include religious values, general virtues, and categories of people. Have the congregation complete the survey to identify their five top values of those listed. You can offer them an opportunity to specify one "other" value not on the list. This will reveal the <u>aspirational</u> values of your congregation. Write down your top aspirational values.

Report the outcome of the survey to the congregation. Then, have your vision team take the top three to five or so values identified by the survey and the top three to five values from your analysis of the practiced values data and build a list of eight to ten values that capture both your actual practiced values and your congregational aspirations. These will be the values that actually typify your congregation.

Most importantly, the values that they currently practice will be the ones leadership will need to use to help them live into their aspirations.

For example, if the aspiration is young people, but the actual current practice is paying attention to those who have been here a long time, you will need to enlist the people who have been here a long time in any strategy to reach younger people. The people and practices currently at the center of focus will need to be the people and practices that you put to work in redirecting focus toward the people and practices you aspire to.

One congregation clearly practiced a value for its older generation members. Its aspirational value was a focus on youth. It started a youth program that included dinner for every weekly youth meeting. The meal was served family style with four or five youth and two "table parents" at each table. Table parents, selected mostly from among the older members, came 10 minutes before dinner, ate with the same kids each week, and led the groups in guided discussion and activities provided for them to use at the table. After dinner the kids went off to other activities and the table parents remained together for another few minutes to share about their kids and pray for them together. Many older adults loved this ministry and became strong advocates and mentors in faith for these young people.

It's all about the mission.

> *Every bit of this book assumes that you are answering these questions about mission, vision and values. As leaders you must see that this most important work is being done.*

Every bit of this book assumes that you are answering these questions about mission, vision and values. As leaders you must see that this most important work is being done. It requires an intimate and evolving relationship with scripture, especially the gospels and book of Acts. It requires deepening relationship with God through both personal and gathered prayer and worship. It requires a spiritual relationship with one another in the congregation through persistent and honest holy conversation. Nothing else matters if you have not done it. Every time you see that word *mission* again ask yourself, "Do I - do we - know what our mission is?"

Study Questions

1. What is the mission, or motivating purpose, of your congregation?

2. How does your church make this mission clear to the members of your church and how is it expressed to those who might be interested in becoming one of you?

3. What is the vision of your congregation?

    a. Who are you sent to reach?

    b. What is your definition of a Christian (or a disciple)?

    c. What are the practices you use to help people become that kind of Christian or disciple?

    d. What are the core values of your congregation?

Chapter Two
Leadership Matters

Here is a definition of leadership.

"Leadership is the quality exercised by a person when they empower a group of people to accomplish their mission through a coordinated effort."

That definition is a description not a prescription. Leadership may be spiritual, good, bad, oppressive, liberating, effective, demeaning, ...whatever! Those kinds of terms prescribe what leadership should be. The whole remainder of this book is about how leadership can be spiritual, good, and faithful as well as effective. But when I use the word leadership, I just want you to know that this is what I mean. A leader is, very simply, someone who is empowering a group of people to accomplish a shared mission. Leaders are not a special or higher category of people, they are just people doing a certain category of work in a group of people. There are lots of other categories of work being done by other people in the church, and leaders are neither more nor less valuable or honor-worthy than the people doing all the rest of it.

Neither do I consider "leadership" or "leaders" to be an *optional* part of a community of people. I know that there is a lot of interest today in "leaderless movements." The Occupy Movement and The Arab Spring were two examples of what are often called leaderless movements, but I think calling them leaderless movements is misleading. If they are truly leaderless, then I doubt there will be any movement. These may be groups where leadership is performed with new and different tools and in perhaps unprecedented ways. But there are leaders. And the art is the same even if the tools are changing. Group effort will always require facilitation and coordination - leadership.

If there is a bunch of people who understand themselves to be a community, no matter how fuzzy their sense of that may be, then there is at least one leader among them (probably a whole network of leaders) and leadership is being done.

Perhaps an ordinary example will help.

There was a church that had an annual kid's carnival.
I asked congregational leaders, "Who is the leader of your annual carnival?"
They energetically exclaim, "No one! We just all do it together!"
So, say I, "How did this year's date for the event get set?"
They answer, "Ginger called the office and put it on the calendar."
"But," I reply, "When did you plan the event?"
They respond, "Ginger announced in worship that interested people should meet at coffee hour and we went from there."
"How about all those details," I ask, "How did you arrange to rent the bouncy house?"
One in the group says, as they all nod their heads, "Ginger asked Fred to call and order it. Fred got his normal group of guys together to set it up."

All this proves, of course, that despite their protest that there was no leader - there *was* a leader. Everyone seems to call her "Ginger." The leader coordinated the group so that a date got set, a planning meeting was scheduled, and a myriad of tasks were assigned to workers who accomplished them. "Ginger" was the leader. She even commissioned another leader, Fred, who organized the bouncy house part.

If something has happened, there was probably a leader. This does not mean the leader did it. It means the leader "...facilitated a group of people in accomplishing a mission through a coordinated effort." If there is no leader, it is very unlikely a mission will be accomplished. Without a leader, a collection of people might not even discover that they have a mission!

It is also worth saying that an effectively led group of people is powerful. They have impact on the people in the group and on others, sometimes many others. The problem for us is that groups of people can be effectively led in ways that are a blessing to them and to the world, but they can also be led effectively in ways that are a curse. This can even happen in a church!

If people who seek to fulfill the will of God for themselves and their neighbors fail to lead in ways that bless, then we leave it to others whose intentions may be less benevolent, and those others are always busy. As Edmund Burke said so well, "All that is necessary for evil to triumph is for good men [and women] to do nothing." Leaders of evil and selfish intent will step in where there is insufficient or ineffective leadership of good and selfless intent.

That is why leadership matters. That is why the modifiers we attach to the word leadership also matter. They matter a lot.

Leadership can be empowering, ethical, and fruitful. Leadership can also be oppressive, immoral, and death dealing. Impactful, influential groups have leaders. Blessed groups have leaders who help them accomplish blessed ends through means that are empowering and life-giving. The answer to bad leaders is not no leaders - it's good leaders.

What are the qualities of good leaders?

Later we will talk about some specific ways to identify and develop leaders in your church, but it will be helpful at the beginning to talk about some of the things that good church leaders have in common, no matter what kind of group they are leading.

Good church leaders are motivated by the calling of Christ and the mission of the group they are leading.

Too often in our culture (and in our churches) we have acted as though leadership is about recognition or honor. Our United Methodist Discipline even says that, "...the charge conference may make provision *for the recognition of the faithful service* of members of the church council by electing them *honorary* members." (Para. 246.3 emphasis mine) I can't even begin to express how sad it makes me that we say stuff like that in our Discipline. Unfortunately, the charge conference, which is the core leadership body of the local United Methodist congregation, recommends recognition and honor as reasons for being in a position of leadership. It assumes that placement in a position of leadership is some kind of reward.

There is no clause in the Discipline stating that the charge conference may make provision for the recognition of the faithful service of members by electing them to weed the flower garden or teach the middle school boys, or volunteer in the local food bank, so one can only assume that being asked to serve in those ways is no such honor or recognition, while being on the charge conference is.

> *If there is no leader, you can be assured there will be no accomplishment of a mission.*

That attitude about leadership, of course, completely ignores what Jesus said about leadership.

> *"But Jesus called them to him and said, 'You know that the rulers of the Gentiles lord it over them, and their great ones are tyrants over them. It will not be so among you; but whoever wishes to be great among you must be your servant, and whoever wishes to be first among you must be your slave; just as the Son of Man came not to be served but to serve, and to give his life a ransom for many.'" (Matthew 25:20-28)*

What Jesus said about good leadership was that it is work (servants do work) and that this work is for the benefit of others (servants - guess what? - serve). Honor and recognition are about the ego of the leader, and that is the way of the world not the way of discipleship. Good church leaders are people who know what mission Jesus has assigned to their church and they want nothing more from their service than that the mission should be fulfilled. Good church leaders do not care about honors, they care about the mission.

I don't want to lie. It feels pretty good when people honor me for what I have done for and with them. When I turned fifty the church I was serving honored me with a surprise party to celebrate my birthday and the twentieth anniversary of my ordination. It felt good. I choked up to see all these people who were telling me that, somehow, I had brought a blessing to them. To say that good leaders are motivated by calling and mission is not to imply that they do not have feelings. Leaders need to hear, "Good job! Thanks for all you do!" But that is true for everyone who serves the mission, not just leaders.

All of us, not just leaders, need feedback indicating when we have been faithful and useful. This is no more or less true for leaders than it is for the person who weeds the church flower garden or teaches the middle school boys. Everyone in the church, no matter what role they play in the fulfilling of the mission, will be strengthened and blessed when their service is recognized and appreciated. Good leaders will make sure this happens!

But all people in the church, leaders and workers alike, will do good and blessed work only when they do it out of devotion to the calling of Christ and the mission of the Body of Christ. It will all go wrong if our motives are rooted in a desire for honor and reward. This is what Jesus was talking about when he said,

> "Do you thank the slave for doing what was commanded? So, you also, when you have done all that you were ordered to do, say, 'We are worthless slaves; we have done only what we ought to have done!'" (Luke 17:9-10)

Of course, he was making the point very strikingly, but the

point is that it's not about honor and recognition. What we do as disciples is all about fulfilling the mission that we have in Christ Jesus.

All people can play a role in the mission of Jesus Christ, whether they are in a leadership calling, a helper calling, a teaching calling, or any other of the almost infinite roles that faithful disciples can fulfill. And all of these people will find their greatest reward if they seek recognition most fervently in Christ and his calling. That is why Jesus also said,

> *"Well done, good and trustworthy slave! Because you have been trustworthy in a few things, I will put you in charge of many things; enter into the joy of your master."*
>
> *(Matthew 25:21)*

Good church leaders do not do it on their own.

When the planning is being done, leaders are not the people who say, "I can do that." They are the people who say, "Which one of you will do that?"

I love people who get things done. I like to be seen as a person who gets things done. But leaders must have as their first priority helping others get things done. Obviously, somebody needs to do it, whatever it is. But if you put people in leadership who always say, "I got that," bad things happen.
First, everyone else who cares about that ministry will slowly drift back and step out because they will feel disconnected from the mission that inspired them.

Second, the growth of the ministry will cease when it reaches the capacity of one person (the "leader") to get it done. When the leader does it instead of coordinating a group in doing it, ministry will devolve down to everyone just doing something they personally want to do, and no one will be participating in the mission of the group. (At that point it is legitimate to ask whether they are a congregation at all, or just a bunch of people who haven't yet gotten into a big enough conflict to look for somewhere else to do what they want.)

Besides, doing it yourself completely ignores what Jesus taught us about leadership.

> *When it was evening on that day, the first day of the week, and the doors of the house where the disciples had met were locked for fear of the Jews, Jesus came and stood among them and said, "Peace be with you." After he said this, he showed them his hands and his side. Then the disciples rejoiced when they saw the Lord. Jesus said to them again, "Peace be with you. As the Father has sent me, so I send you." (John 20:19-21)*

And in case you don't remember, practically the next thing he did was to ascend into heaven and leave them to go get it done!

Jesus sent others to do what he taught them to do. Jesus led and empowered others. If he trusted us to carry out his mission, certainly we ought to be able to trust our brothers and sisters to carry out our congregation's part of the mission!

> **When the planning is being done, leaders are not the people who say, "I can do that." They are the people who say, "Which one of you will do that?"**

This practice of leaders trusting the mission to others results in multiplication.

Leaders enlist others in working out the mission, and ultimately this means that the work gets multiplied far beyond the capacity of the leader. It's one of the things John Wesley excelled in. It is also evident in the promise Jesus made to Andrew, *"You will see greater things than these!" (John 1:50)*

Good church leaders lead and live in ways that give glory to Christ.

Good church leaders lead and live in the service of Jesus' values and mission. You are welcome to have any discussion you like about what the values and mission of Jesus are. I would refer you to the Gospels and to a lively conversation with others in your congregation. I trust you'll come up with something that will lead you in the right direction. But there are definitely no disciples, and the group is not Christians, if their purpose together is not to embody and extend the Way of Jesus Christ.

Good church leaders are spiritual leaders. They are disciples of Jesus who lead, and a disciple is a person who is learning from a master. Good church leaders, therefore, are people who practice the disciplines of a disciple. They have a prayer life that penetrates their daily life. They have a worship discipline that keeps them fully engaged in the life of the whole congregation (Body of Christ). They are regularly employed in service to the community beyond the church. And they support the mission of the church financially as they are able (and no one is not able at all!). Fruitful congregations are places where the whole body (even those who do not do these things!) expects their leaders to be people who do these things.

Good leaders seek to remain true to the specific call of Christ upon their own particular lives.

Good leaders have many things in common with each other, but one thing they do not have in common is a responsibility to all accomplish the exact same things. One good leader excels at getting people together for a great time of fellowship and deepening relationship. Another leader is driven by a desire to see that needy people have food. Hopefully you have a leader who is excited by the opportunity to share money and to help others grow to become generous givers to accomplish great things for Christ. These people are no more "interchangeable" than are your workers who do plumbing, decorating, singing, or cooking.

Leaders accomplish their absolute best work when they are devoted to the particular ministry they are leading. (This principle actually applies to both leaders and doers; they all thrive best and accomplish the most when they are performing out of a sense of personal calling.) Serving in a calling never sounds like, "I guess it's my turn," or, "If no one else is willing." On the other hand, it also never sounds like, "I only do things that are fun or rewarding for me." Effective leaders engage out of a clear sense that God wants them to do what they are doing. This requires that they take seriously two things:

- What interests me, excites me, motivates me, and energizes me?
- What does God want to see happen in the church and the world because I'm here?

True calling is found at the intersection of these two realities. Often the intersection includes things we would rather not have to do, but we know them to be part of the bigger purpose that God has placed upon us.

We'll look some more at leadership later, but these ideas should be held in mind as we move forward. Everything else we say about organization and leadership will be based on these ideas about leaders and leadership. We will try to organize the church so that these are the kinds of leaders we get. And we will try to organize the church in ways that make the most of this kind of leadership.

What are the qualities of groups that support good leadership?

We often assume that good leaders create good groups, but the relationship between good leaders and good groups is much more complicated and dynamic than that.

It turns out that leaders can't be good leaders if they are not doing their work in good congregations. Congregations often make mistakes around leadership that interfere with their ability to fulfill their mission. When congregations expect the wrong things of their leaders or place them in the wrong positions, the group will not function well no matter how capable their leaders are. Let's look at some of the common mistakes that many congregations make regarding leadership.

Churches may seek the wrong qualities in the selection of leaders.

Churches frequently select people as leaders for the wrong reasons. People are often asked to be leaders in order to honor them, because of loyal service, or simply because "no one else was willing." We have all experienced the problems that result when someone who is not equipped to lead in a given situation is asked to take the lead.

That person may not be the right person because they lack the ability, or the interest, or the time; but it really won't matter why - if the person in leadership is not equipped and called for that responsibility, the mission of the group will not be effectively fulfilled. Asking someone ill-equipped to lead in a particular situation will often result in bad feelings in the group and a sense of failure for everyone involved. But leaders themselves also suffer when they are in the wrong position. It is far too common to see someone asked to lead in a capacity they are ill prepared to fulfill and having such a demeaning and painful experience that they chose to leave the church.

Groups need to take seriously that there are a very limited number of people in any particular group who are really best equipped (and called) to be the leader in any particular situation. We even need to consider not doing something at all if we don't have someone called and equipped to lead it.

Anywhere Community Church was frustrated that its Sunday morning children's program continued its slow but relentless decline. Young families occasionally visited for a few weeks and reported that they liked the people, but inevitably they moved on to find a congregation with a better children's program.

Church members frequently expressed disappointment about this. The pastor hinted on various occasions

> *We often assume that good leaders create good groups, but the relationship between good leaders and good groups is much more complicated and dynamic than that.*

that maybe they needed a new Sunday School Superintendent, but she was repeatedly discouraged from recruiting someone new because, "Sam has been serving in this position for 20 years and it would break his heart to be replaced, and besides, no one is more devoted to the program than he is. He shows up at 5:30 on Sunday mornings to prepare the curriculum for all the classes, and he even teaches the middle school class all by himself since we have been unable to find anyone else willing to do that."

This imaginary story demonstrates a few of our typical errors in leadership deployment. First, let it be noted that Sam loves his church and the Christian education program; there is no question about that. But it is also clear that Sam is more of a helper than a leader. The very qualities mentioned in connection with his service involve him *doing* the work of the ministry and not at all the work of *inspiring and deploying others* in the ministry. In fact, you would undoubtedly hear from Sam (if you asked him) that he really dislikes the recruiting part of the job and that it is usually easier to just do it himself. In addition, the first reason cited to keep Sam in the position is entirely about honoring Sam's loyalty and has nothing to do with the responsibility of the Sunday School Superintendent, which is to lead a group of people in providing a ministry to children that serves the families of the church (and those who might become families of the church).

The hard lesson is that, in assigning leadership this way, the congregation is failing both to put Sam's actual gifts to fruitful use and to fulfill its mission. I can assure you that Sam struggles with frustration at the decline of the program and bears a burden of secret guilt that he is somehow failing his beloved congregation. A fruitful leadership practice would honor Sam's gifts by placing him in a calling that he is suited for and putting someone better suited in the superintendent role.

Sadly, it is likely that because we have taught everyone, including Sam, that leadership is an *honor*, he will of course be hurt and feel *dishonored* if he is replaced in the leadership role even though it is giving him guilt and frustration. A vital and well-led church will make the change because the mission requires it. Sam will be deployed in a ministry where he can be successful, and the mission is supported.

Churches often ask effective leaders to lead in the wrong leadership positions.

This happens when churches consider leadership to be a kind of generic talent, so that they believe that someone is either a leader or not, without regard to the specific ministry that is at stake. In truth the ability of a particular person to lead effectively depends on the specific situation in which they are leading. The fruitfulness of the leader will be dependent on what kinds of purposes and activities that particular leader finds compelling. It depends on whether he or she has time for the particular demands of this leadership challenge. It depends on how many people will be in the working group (some people are good at leading large groups and others small ones). When a congregation deploys its limited number of able leaders as though they can simply be plugged in anywhere they make a grave mistake about how leadership actually works.

Congregations may make the mistake of using their highest potential leaders in ministries that have little significance for the mission of the church. This is especially likely to happen with legacy programs that are no longer relevant, but still cherished in the congregation.

One of the characteristics that are usually present in high potential leaders is that they have an innate desire to help the group they are leading make a meaningful difference. If congregations, as they so often do, keep high-potential new leaders in low-impact situations for too long, they will inevitably lose the leadership of these people. Effective leaders want to make a difference, and they will take their abilities to groups that are willing to ask them to accomplish significant and meaningful purposes. Here's an example:

George is an executive at the local bank and a devoted member of his church as well as a significant financial supporter. Naturally,

> *Vital congregations call leaders who have proven effectiveness relevant to the leadership position they are asked to accept, and then they follow the lead of those leaders.*

when the congregation's treasurer of 20 years moved away the nominating committee thought of George. When they approached him about taking the position he asked a few questions about what it entailed and was assured that it would not be too burdensome, and that they really needed him. He said something about it not being his thing really, but if no one else was willing, he guessed he could do it. That sounded like, "yes," to the nominating committee and he was elected at the next board meeting. The following day the pastor called to congratulate him and arrange a meeting to turn the books over to him.

A lot of profound opportunity was missed in that very typical story of leadership development. George is actually an executive at the bank because of his ability to inspire and coordinate the efforts of a large and diverse group of people: tellers, janitors, middle management people, human relations managers, (and, uhm, accountants and bookkeepers) - to effectively serve the purpose of the bank. George has also had a long-time personal aspiration to do something about the low-income housing shortage in his community, but the nominating committee never asked him about his aspirations.

As it turns out, George is not very knowledgeable about bookkeeping, and not at all interested in it. The church sees "treasurer" as a significant leadership position, but the treasurer's responsibility does not require inspiring people to get involved in the outreach of the church. In fact, while it is a very important job in the life of the church, it is not a leadership position at all in terms of "facilitating and coordinating the efforts of a group of people to serve a mission." The treasurer's (very important) job is to write the checks, keep the books in good order, and provide useful accurate financial information to the congregation.

George will undoubtedly do his best to be a good treasurer for the church he loves. It will not feed his soul. And it will not inspire his congregation. If, on the other hand, the nominating committee had bothered to learn what George is really good at and what his dreams are, they may well have done something different. They may have hired a bookkeeping service. They may have asked George to lead a new Habitat for Humanity ministry team that, given George's abilities and calling, might well be providing houses to multiple families in the community and serving as an open door into the church for those in the community who are inspired by George's mission to serve.

The lesson is that, in assigning leadership this way, the congregation is failing both to utilize George's actual gifts and to fulfill its mission. A fruitful leadership practice would honor George's gifts by placing him in a calling that he is passionate about, and by caring for the tasks of the treasurer in some other way.

Churches may expect their leaders to do the wrong things.

In our old-line denominational congregations, this mistake usually takes the form of expecting leaders today to do the same things in the same way our leaders did twenty (no – sixty!) years ago. It can also occur when groups expect their leader to do it for them instead of coordinating them in doing it themselves. This is true in many congregations around the basic disciplines like worship, prayer, immersion in scripture, sharing the faith, and serving our neighbor. Indeed, in modern American mainline Protestantism it is hard to think of a practice intended for every Christian that has not been taken away from ordinary Christian people and put onto the shoulders of Christian leaders.

For centuries one of the distinguishing marks of a Christian community was that the people in them cared for one another. Jesus taught about this when he said to his followers,

"I give you a new commandment, that you love one another. Just as I have loved you, you also should love one another. By this everyone will know that you are my disciples, if you have love for one another." (John 13:34-35)

In John Wesley's Methodist Societies what we now call "pastoral care" was entirely done for one another by the people in the Methodist classes. Somehow the care of the members of the church has shifted away from, "we all care for one another," to, "we'll call the pastor to come see you."

Part of my job description as a new United Methodist Associate Pastor was to care for the shut-ins in the congregation. When I would visit with them I was often told, "It was so nice of you to come, Pastor Steve, but I wish the minister would come." When even an associate pastor is not considered a representative of the church, you can bet that the members of the church are not being seen as the church. We have actually managed to teach people that if the preacher has not called on them, then the church has not ministered to them! This expectation completely fails to acknowledge the "priesthood of all believers."

Whatever the particular source of a congregation's failure to thrive, congregations that are failing in their mission are almost always wrong about what to do about that failure. Our church people mostly want their churches to succeed in the mission of extending the faith. The most common reason for our congregations to decline is that good and faithful people are doing the wrong things. So, it is truly amazing how easy it is for a group of people to recruit someone as their leader because that person has been successful in the endeavor for which they have been recruited, but then refuse to implement any of the insight that the leader is bringing them!

If everyone in a group, or even just a very committed and demanding minority, are wrong about what is needed, there will be very little that that ANY leader can do to help that group achieve its mission. Vital congregations call leaders who have proven effectiveness relevant to the leadership position they are asked to accept, and then they follow the lead of those leaders.

Another Community Church struggled for several years to keep their youth group going and finally found it was no longer able even to get anyone to volunteer to serve as youth leader for the six kids in their high school group. Fortunately, one of the members knew of a young woman, Judy, who was just returning to town from college and who had served as a youth minister a student there. He had heard good things about her youth ministry, so he gathered three or four other members and together they approached the pastor to announce they were prepared to commit enough money to hire Judy ten hours a week at minimum wage to be their youth leader. Everything fell into place. Judy started in August.

It didn't take long before things began to fall apart, however. Judy wanted to scrap the weekly Sunday evening fellowship group and replace it with a menu of options for teenagers. She planned to offer a teen "Bible experience" on Sunday mornings (during the worship service), a monthly Friday evening "celebration fellowship," quarterly local mission and service events, and an annual spring break mission trip.

The current six kids were mixed in their reaction. Some liked Judy and her ideas, but a couple of them wanted their good old weekly Sunday evening fellowship group and nothing else. New kids, few of them from church families, became the primary participants in the service activities. Several of the long-time members criticized the Friday fun events as "just parties" and when one of the funding partners visited one he didn't recognize any of the fifteen kids there. Fundraising for the mission events seemed like a constant irritating drone to some of the regular members. And, yeah, they really wanted to see all the youth in worship on Sunday morning.

By May the small group who funded Judy's position met with the pastor to express their concerns that what Judy was doing really didn't fit with their expectations or what they understood to be the needs of the congregation. In June the pastor announced Judy's intention to move on to somewhere else, and an opening for a new youth leader. Nobody really talked much about the fact that there were 26 kids and 9 adults on the spring break mission trip.

The hard lesson is that, in assigning leadership this way, the congregation is failing both to honor Judy's actual gifts and to fulfill its mission. A fruitful leadership practice would make use of Judy's gifts by supporting an effective leader in implementing change in a program that was proven to be failing, and by celebrating the early successes evident in fulfilling the purposes for which she was called.

OK. We get it. What can we do about it?

What are the fruitful leadership practices of good groups? Fortunately, they are simple to understand. Unfortunately, they are hard to practice. That is why most groups have a very hard time accomplishing what they intend.

Study Questions

1. Bring to mind someone you have known personally and greatly respected as a church leader. Which qualities were present in that person?

    a. Was devoted to Christ and to the mission of our church?

    b. Inspired others to devote themselves to Christ and the mission of the church?

    c. Lead and lived in ways that exemplified the values of Christ?

    d. Focused his or her efforts in ways that expressed his or her specific gifts and graciously declined other opportunities to lead?

    e. Other qualities?

2. Recall a time when you observed someone struggling in a church leadership position. Which of the following errors in use of leaders might have contributed to that difficulty?

    a. The wrong qualities were sought in recruiting the leader?

    b. A good leader was placed in the wrong position?

    c. The congregation expected the leader to do things that were not fruitful in the responsibility they were assigned?

    d. Other reasons?

Chapter Three
Principles of Effective Leadership

For a fuller account of the principles and practices of an "accountable leadership system" you may look to Edmund Kaiser, "Winning On Purpose: How to Organize Congregations to Succeed In Their Mission." That is where these ideas were formulated. I have adapted these ideas from Kaiser to make them more accessible to the people in my church tradition.

For any congregation to experience excellent and effective leadership they must first agree that leadership is important, and that calling the right people into leadership is worth significant attention and effort. Once the congregation agrees that it must make effective use of good leadership there are three elements that will be part of its culture and practice of leadership. All three elements must be present, and they must be mixed in the right proportions. The three elements are Responsibility, Authority, and Accountability.

These are the elements of a leadership practice that must be present and aligned if your congregation is to have a reasonable chance of accomplishing its mission. Using adequate structures of organization will help us to attend to these elements as we identify and deploy leaders, but no structure can ever guarantee that we will not ignore one or another of them when it is difficult or inconvenient to keep them all in place. For now, we need to focus like a laser on these three foundational elements of a fruitful leadership system.

Responsibility

Responsibility refers to a clear description of the specific outcome the congregation is seeking.

How can someone lead, or a group succeed, if they do not know what they are trying to accomplish? It seems obvious, but in practice this is frequently overlooked.

When a ministry or activity has been in place for a long time the purpose that originally motivated it and, thus, the responsibility of those who lead it, is often lost. Ask an elected leader in your church, "What are you responsible for accomplishing with and for the people you lead?" Many leaders will tell you they are not sure. In fact, often our church leaders will not even be able to identify the people that they are supposed to be leading. When this is the case, clearly the responsibility is obscure, and leaders are at a loss in knowing what the mission is.

Sometimes leaders will be able to articulate what they are supposed to accomplish, but it doesn't reflect a *leadership* responsibility. There are many roles in a vital church that are essential, but that are not leadership. Leadership involves coordinating a group of people in accomplishing a mission. When churches have great job descriptions written for everyone, but they have made no meaningful distinction between leadership responsibilities and ministry responsibilities, they will lose the ability to coordinate the whole action of the congregation toward a focused vision, mission or purpose. Everyone will know what he or she is supposed to do, but no one will know how or why he or she is supposed to fit with anyone else in the mission of the church. A leadership responsibility will always describe the group that leader is supposed to coordinate and, the specific ministry they are to accomplish, and how that participates in the mission / vision of the congregation.

Even when leaders can answer the mission question in terms of a group effort, their answer will often be very task-oriented with no clear missional

> *When a ministry or activity has been in place for a long time the purpose that originally motivated it and, thus, the responsibility of those who lead it, is often lost.*

or purposeful content. If the responsibility of the leader is "to coordinate the annual bazaar" the responsibility (by itself) fails to articulate an outcome. Is that a fundraiser? How much do they need to raise? What will the funds be used for? Is that a fellowship event? Who is supposed to enjoy this fellowship? Is that event designed to help members engage with people outside the church? Is it an occasion to celebrate the creative abilities of the members? Is it a way of transferring good stuff from people who have more than they need to other people who have less than they need?

If the shared intent of the bazaar is several or maybe even all of these purposes, what is the order of priority? And, especially important, how does the specific purpose of this ministry support and extend the overall mission of the whole congregation? What does it have to do with the mission of Christ through your congregation?

These questions are important because if the purpose is really fundraising, it will not matter how creative you are or how much fun you had, or how many people got cheap stuff unless you made some money. And if leaders do not know the **purpose** of the ministries they are asked to lead, they are likely to make an awful lot of wrong choices as they try to coordinate and align their group. A leadership responsibility will always clearly state what outcome is desired as a result of the ministry group being led.

The responsibility should also be clear about who the ministry is designed to benefit. Is the bazaar primarily intended to benefit the church by raising funds from the community? Or, is it precisely the opposite - is it designed to benefit the people of the community outside the church by providing them with a nice holiday experience and some decorations at bargain prices? Who is supposed to benefit, and what is that benefit intended to be? And if there are several answers (which is fine!) again, what, are the priorities? A leadership responsibility should always state who is supposed to benefit and what is the benefit intended.

Now, you may say, "Everyone knows what the bazaar is (and what it is about)." Maybe everyone who has been here for 20 years does. But new people may have no clue. In fact, a good number of your regular participants have no clue. Just ask them. You'll get all of the above answers and a few more besides. If we are not explicit about the responsibility that is borne by the bazaar ministry group, then it will have a bad impact on leadership and outcome.

When the purpose of a ministry is unclear new people will not be welcome to participate in the ministry. How can people become involved in something if no one can tell them what it is for? Worse, we may actually engage new leaders and helpers (usually by telling them it will be fun or that they should help) and then criticize them for doing it wrong. Lack of clarity about the purpose also results in conflicts between participants who may have divergent assumptions about what they are supposed to be doing. And, since it is purpose that energizes people in action, a lack of clear responsibility also results in apathy about getting things done.

You cannot have effective and fruitful leadership if your congregation does not do the necessary work of getting clear about what the real purposes are that drive the activities and ministries it asks people to lead and to support. For this reason, really effective leaders will tend to insist on clarity about their responsibility. They will not be motivated by a simple task list (which is a job description for a helper, not a leader). Effective leaders often refuse to start leading until they have gotten the group to provide a clear sense of the direction they want to go.

Churches that want to experience the vitality that effective leadership empowers will talk enough about what they are trying to accomplish to make clear statements about the responsibility that they assign to every leadership role.

A clear statement of responsibility will answer the following questions:
- Who are the people whose lives are to benefit from this ministry or activity? (Hint: "everyone" is not an answer.)

> *You cannot have effective and fruitful leadership if your congregation does not do the necessary work of getting clear about what the real purposes are that drive the activities and ministries it asks people to lead and to support.*

•What is the benefit that we intend them to receive?

•How will we know (when we have done it) whether or not those people received that benefit?

•What are the limits or boundaries within which the ministry is free to work in accomplishing these ends (funding, facilities, timeframes, values, etc.)?

• How does this responsibility contribute to the fulfillment of our overall mission as a congregation?

Responsibility statements do not need to be simple. Indeed, they may be somewhat complex, including multiple communities of benefit. The bazaar may, for example, benefit the creative people who enjoy an opportunity to share their creations with others, the community of people around the church who receive a holiday experience and reasonably priced decorations and goodies, and the mission of the congregation as it collects email addresses of families with children to be invited to the Christmas pageant. But responsibility statements must be clear and should provide priorities when there are multiple purposes and communities of benefit.

Authority

Authority is the authorization to do any things necessary, consistent with the values and resources of our congregation, to accomplish the stated responsibility.

Authority is derived from the group, not imposed on it. Authority is a delegation to the leader of whatever will be necessary to focus the combined efforts of the group effectively toward the responsibility.

> *... separating authority from responsibility serves to make sure that we keep doing things the way that worked in the past.*

This is a critical issue for most of our mainline congregations, because often we intentionally separate authority from responsibility. Authority is separated from responsibility by requiring that a group that is not responsible for accomplishing the ministry (a committee, council, or even the whole church) grant approval before the people actually responsible can take actions required to fulfill their responsibility.

For example, the worship team is generally responsible for providing passionate worship experiences for the congregation. However, the staff committee or church council does the hiring and firing of the paid musician. The church council or even an all-church vote must be obtained before there can be any change in worship time or the number of worship services. The worship team that actually plans and leads worship every week does not have the authority required to coordinate and lead passionate worship.

Yet, if worship participation has been steadily declining, no one blames the church council or all-church meeting. They blame the pastor and worship leaders. No church council (or entire congregation) ever resigned in shame over a 20-year decline in worship attendance, but churches often have recommended a change in pastoral leadership every four or five years. This is a very clear separation of responsibility from authority.

The authority necessary to fulfill the responsibility of providing passionate worship would certainly include the ability to select the music, and to decide what musicians are best suited to providing the support of that music. It would certainly include the authority to set (even experiment with) different times of worship and numbers of services. These authorities would not mean that the worship team is not answerable to the congregation. Granting these authorities to the worship team would mean that they are answerable to the congregation for providing passionate worship instead of for checking off a list of worship experiences and activities determined by the council or staff committee.

In our churches we have practiced the separation of responsibility and authority for two *legitimate* reasons. First, *separating authority from responsibility serves to make sure that we keep doing things the way that has worked in the past.* When the people responsible for a ministry do not have the authority to make changes, then permission is always assumed to be present only for doing the same things we've done before in ways we did them before. No worship team ever needed council approval *not* to change the time or place of worship. No congregation ever voted whether to allow the use of music from the hymnal. But the process for getting permission to do anything new or different makes it very clear that those responsible for carrying out a ministry do not have the authority to introduce anything new in order to enhance the outcome of a ministry.

When authority and responsibility are separated, those responsible need the permission of others, even of people who have nothing to do the with the ministry in question, in order to act to fulfill their responsibility. Separating authority from responsibility serves to strengthen the status quo.

Let's use an example from the history of my denomination to illustrate how authority and responsibility get separated to preserve an effective practice.

> *Authority is derived from the group, not imposed on it. Authority is a delegation to the leader of whatever will be necessary to focus the combined efforts of the group effectively toward the missional responsibility.*

John Wesley was an Anglican priest who felt called to spread personal and social holiness among the people of The Church of England. He and his brother Charles began to practice some radically new ways of doing worship including new hymns and hymn tunes and preaching in fields and other secular spaces.

That didn't go over well with the leaders of their denomination. In fact, Wesley was soon denied the right to lead worship in the Churches of England. He was clearly judged to have exceeded his authority regarding the provision of worship for the people and was denied the opportunity to lead worship in the approved spaces.

This happened despite the fact that he was leading thousands of de-churched people in worship while most established churches were nearly empty (the standard of the day for retaining membership in The Church of England was attendance in worship once a year). Thankfully he continued to lead worship anyway, by taking it wherever the people could gather.

Because Wesley persisted in *taking* the authority to fulfill his sense of responsibility, this new way of doing worship soon proved so successful that many Methodist preachers were leading worship the way Wesley did. They requested, and Wesley provided for them, a standard Sunday Service and a list of approved hymns. That Standard Sunday Service and approved hymnal required that they do worship the way he had. They were happy to do so, since it worked so well in fulfilling their shared intention of spreading personal and social holiness.

Did you notice what happened in that story? When Wesley went out to spread personal and social holiness, he took the authority to do whatever he felt he needed to in order to accomplish that end and devised new ways of leading worship. When that way of leading worship proved fruitful and effective, the Methodists removed the authority of preachers to innovate in worship (as Wesley had), while leaving them <u>responsible</u> for spreading scriptural and social holiness.

They separated the authority to lead worship from the responsibility to provide worship. In fact, they standardized many other ministry practices such as preaching, small group practice and other specifics of their way of being church. It was working, so it was smart to prevent risky innovation by taking authority away while leaving the responsibility in place. We separate authority from responsibility in order to suppress innovation when what we are doing is working well.

> *Rogues and loose cannons can make our whole group look bad. To protect our corporate credibility, we keep adding more and more safety devices around our leaders.*

"If it ain't broke, don't fix it."

The second reason that groups separate authority from responsibility is to protect the integrity of the group. Sometimes empowering someone with the authority to go and get "it" done results in people taking risks or making mistakes that cause our whole group to look bad. It doesn't really matter whether those leaders are malicious or just mistaken; when this happens, it can deal a severe blow to our ability to fulfill our mission.

Rogues and loose cannons can make our whole group look bad. To protect our corporate credibility, we keep adding more and more safety devices around our leaders. We make policies and rules about how to do things. We also add layers of oversight and approval before anyone can act (we separate authority from responsibility). Eventually nobody can actually do anything unless we have already done it before or unless everybody in our group has approved.

Most churches have had bad experiences with giving people authority and then having them make the whole group look bad. Think Roman Catholic Church abuse scandals, Jimmy Swaggert, Jim and Tammy Faye Bakker, and Jim Jones. These are all instances where leaders with authority to do as they pleased have caused significant damage to the groups they led. Every group eventually experiences these kinds of problems.

We have responded to these kinds of bad experiences in our mainline denominations by devising leadership qualification systems that take years to complete. Even after we ordain leaders we surround them with literally hundreds of rules limiting the authority of these presumably highly pre-qualified people. Wesley approved his pastors on the basis of a few conversations and references from people who had experienced the impact of their leadership. He also removed people from service pretty readily if their performance was not up to his expectations!

> *Sometimes empowering someone with the authority to go and get "it" done results in people taking risks or making mistakes that cause our whole group look bad.*

The extreme caution we exercise before granting even limited authority to leaders extends to lay leadership as well. I once sat with the nominating committee of a congregation of about seventy people that decided a certain "young" man was not "ready" to serve as the church council chair. He was forty years old, had been an active member of the congregation for ten years, and was a principal in the local middle school responsible for overseeing the staff of sixty or eighty people and the education of about 500 children. What would it take for us to be able to grant to our leaders the authority required to meet their responsibilities?

While these reasons for limiting authority may have some legitimacy in retaining best practices and protecting our integrity, they also have the effect of neutralizing leadership. In a context *where what we have been doing is working* this way of containing the risks of delegating authority is acceptable.

But our mainline protestant denominations are now in the fifth decade of failure in the way we have been doing things. We need innovative ministries that are able to nimbly change as our world changes in order to remain fruitful in our mission. We need leaders who can coordinate groups of people in imagining and trying new ways of "doing church." That means we need leaders to whom we entrust legitimate authority. We need more leaders like John Wesley and we do not allow, let alone encourage, this kind of leadership when we separate authority from responsibility.

Capable and effective leaders tend to find it very disheartening to be asked to lead a group of people in a ministry and then be required to ask multiple other groups for approval of every detail. These kinds of leaders find it even more discouraging to be given a responsibility and then find they are bound by strategies and practices that have been failing to fulfill that responsibility for more than a generation.

Vital churches make the responsibility in terms of outcome clear. They recruit leaders who show promise to fulfill the responsibility and they grant them the authority to recruit team members and to establish the times, places and practices that will make fulfilling the responsibility reasonably likely.

But how can we protect our group integrity?

Accountability

Accountability is the process by which the leader (and by extension the group of people he or she is leading) knows how success will be determined, who will be keeping track of success, and what limits have been placed on the means by which he or she may pursue fulfilling the responsibility accepted.

One of the less impressive things about human nature is that most of us will not do difficult things if no one else is likely to notice whether or not we actually get them done. It is very helpful for most of us to be held accountable in some way for following through. In the workplace the accountabilities are pretty simple. We need the paycheck. But in our churches, almost all our leaders and doers are volunteers. How can accountability work in our congregations?

As it turns out, accountability does not need to be as coercive as the threat of being fired. If people are leading and serving in ways that honor their calling (gifts and passion) and if they are doing something that matters to them (meaningful and rewarding) then accountability really just boils down to someone asking them if they are following through. It sometimes means asking how it could work better if it's not going well. And it certainly means acknowledging and celebrating success.

Several years ago, I was pastor of a congregation involved in a once-in-a-generation building project. Of

> *Some people are able on their own initiative to persist and overcome these difficulties, but it is very helpful for most of us to be held accountable in some way for following through.*

course, we needed to raise a lot of money. We hired a fund-raising firm to assist us. They provided us with a terrific and detailed plan for the whole three-month process.

During that period the consultant flew in about every three weeks on a Wednesday and met with the leader of each work team (advance gifts, celebration dinner, weekly speakers, and so on). The meeting with each leader lasted about fifteen minutes and consisted of the consultant asking the leader if they had completed the work designated by that date in their area of responsibility. He praised when steps were completed, offered help when they were struggling, and asked, "why not?" when tasks were simply not done. The consultant himself never addressed the congregation during the entire process and worked only with the team leaders.

Being an anxious pastor, I would always ask the team leaders (on the Sunday just before the consultant's next visit) if they were caught up with their responsibilities. The most common answer I received from our team leaders was, "I haven't done it yet but it's on my agenda for this afternoon." As near as I can tell almost all the work in every three-week period happened in three days before each visit of the consultant. I'm glad to be able to report that our leaders did (nearly) everything the plan called for and that we actually raised more money than our goal!

Three years later it was time to do another funding campaign to retire the debt from that same project. We were using the new facilities to full advantage and everyone was very happy with the project. The church was in every way more energized and confident than it had been during the first campaign. When we began to work on the new funding campaign we made a very obvious choice. We had the entire plan the consultant provided for us three years before. We knew how it worked. So why spend $17,000 on the consultant? We could just do it ourselves.

This time when the three-month process had run its course we had actually done about one half of the process, mostly the highly public parts (like the celebration dinner) that everyone would notice if they failed to occur. The harder parts, like recruiting weekly speakers - not so much. We raised about one half what we needed. The biggest difference was that there was no one asking each leader on a regular basis if they were doing what they had said they would do.

Accountability is like magic when it is applied, and it does not need to be rude or unpleasant. Indeed, it works best when people with approximately equivalent responsibilities agree to ask each other at crucial points if they are doing what they set out to do and accomplishing the purpose they were seeking.

In fact - effective leaders tend to do this with one another almost instinctively whenever they get together. It is the best kind of shoptalk. The keys questions for accountability are:

- Is your responsibility clear to you and your team?
- Have you decided on the steps you and your team will take to move toward fulfilling the responsibility? What are those steps? (What is your strategy?)
- Does the team understand the boundaries within which it may act (budget and finance, facilities, timeframes, strategies and appropriate behaviors)?
- Is the team doing the things they have planned to do? If yes - celebrate! If no - why not? Do they need to get busy, or design a more realistic strategy?
- At suitable moments in the process, are the intended outcomes (mission or purposes) being realized?

Accountability is the way we work together faithfully to do ministry the best we can. Certainly, we desire to do our best for Christ who has called us. This means more than simply doing things with excellence. We must also do excellent things! But, no matter how good and godly our intentions may be, excellent ministry is always the result of doing something (even prayer requires praying). I once heard Bill Easum say that, sooner or later, all ministry boils down to work. I have found this to be true in the course of my ministry. St. James said it with more spiritual punch when he wrote to his congregations,

> *What good is it, my brothers and sisters, if you say you have faith but do not have works? Can faith save you? If a brother or sister is naked and lacks daily food, and one of you says to them, "Go in peace; keep warm and eat your*

fill," and yet you do not supply their bodily needs, what is the good of that? So, faith by itself, if it has no works, is dead.

But someone will say, "You have faith and I have works." Show me your faith apart from your works, and I by my works will show you my faith." (James 2:14-18)

Vital churches make the accountability clear. They recruit leaders who are equipped to fulfill the responsibility and they grant them the authority to recruit team members, set times and places and establish practices that will make fulfilling the responsibility reasonably likely. Then vital congregation ask their leaders if they (and their teams) are doing what they set out to do, accomplishing the purposes for which they have been commissioned, and behaving within the boundaries established by the congregation.

Study Questions

1. Consider the element of Responsibility.

   a. How would you describe the responsibility of your current position as a church leader?

   b. Who defined this responsibility for you? (Was it made clear to you before you accepted it? Have you "always known what it was"? Did you have to figure it out by trial and error?)

   c. What are the essential responsibilities of the pastor of your church? (If it's "everything" why is that a problem?)

2. Consider the element of Authority.

   a. What authority have you been entrusted with in order to effectively fulfill your responsibilities in the church?

b. What permissions do you need to obtain from others that inhibit your ability to be fruitful in your responsibility?

3. Consider the element of Accountability.

a. What outcomes of your responsibility are you held accountable for (what are the things that, if they did not happen, you would be asked to step aside)?

b. Who regularly checks in with you to see that you are supported and equipped in fulfilling your responsibility?

c. To whom are you accountable for fruitfulness in your current leadership assignment?

Chapter Four
Governance, Management and Ministry

We have given attention to the practice of leadership. Leadership matters. For leaders to be able to perform fruitfully in the congregation they need to be part of a community that clarifies and aligns responsibility, authority and accountability.

Furthermore, the people who are serving as leaders must be chosen because their gifts and callings are reasonably matched to the responsibility being entrusted to them. Congregations must not select leaders in order to honor or reward them, but according to their gifts and graces. Leaders must strive to be motivated by

> *Governance is the work of leading the whole congregation in discerning and articulating its mission, vision and values. Management is the work of leading and coordinating the specific ministries and responsibilities within the congregation to fulfill the mission. And ministry is the work of directly touching the world with the mission.*

nothing more than the success of the mission Christ has entrusted to them.

Is there a way of organizing our churches that can support that alignment of responsibility, authority and accountability? Yes, but a caution is in order. Organizations are famous for restructuring whenever things aren't going well. The common critique about "rearranging the deck chairs on the Titanic" expresses both our tendency to want to restructure when there is trouble and our well-deserved skepticism that doing so can make any useful difference. Since this is a book about structure, you may well assume that I will defend the idea that re-structuring is a worthwhile endeavor, but I have to tell you that simply changing your organizational chart will not make any difference at all if the way that ministry is *ordered* in the congregation is not transformed.

Ordering, as I am using it here, refers to the way that different kinds of responsibilities get assigned to specific roles within a community. It also has to do with how these various roles are networked with one another as they operate to coordinate the actions of the congregation. Finally, it has to do with helping individuals and groups understand what they are trying to accomplish in the jobs they have been called to, as well as helping them understand how what they do fits into the mission of the congregation as a whole.

So, now we turn to *three basic orders* or categories of service that tend to characterize vital congregations. Vital congregations always have all three of the orders that we will address here. When your congregation intentionally networks these orders of service appropriately it is easier for everyone to function effectively within the congregation. The opposite situation also holds true. When the structure confuses these orders of service or places them in conflict with one another then everyone in the congregation will find that they are often frustrated and seldom effective.

There are three basic orders of service in a vital congregation. Let us call them **governance, management, and ministry**. We begin exploring these orders of serving by reasserting that there is no more honor or value in any one of these than in the others. All three orders of service will be present and valued in a vital congregation. None of them has any significance or virtue apart from their particular role in fulfilling the mission of the church.

The orders of governance and management are where the expression of leadership is most apparent. In a sense, governance is the work of leading the whole congregation in discerning and articulating its mission, vision and values. Management is the work of leading and coordinating the specific ministries and responsibilities within the congregation to fulfill the mission. And ministry is the work of directly touching the world with the mission. Notice that mission is fundamental for all three orders.

The Order of Ministry

We begin with ministry because it is the work closest to the fulfillment of the mission of the congregation.

Ministry is the work that is done in order to directly touch the world with the mission of the congregation here and now.

> *Christians are not "governors, managers or ministers" they are disciples who sometimes do governance, sometimes do management, and always do ministry.*

One of the core ideas of the Christian faith is that Jesus was the *incarnation of* God. Incarnation means "putting it into flesh." Disciples and groups of disciples (congregations) are created by God to incarnate the mission of God in Jesus

Christ. That is what St. Paul meant when he talked about the church as the Body of Christ.

If loving our neighbor as Jesus loved is part of the mission of the church, then ministry is every action of the congregation or its people by which they or their neighbors experience the love of Christ. If nurturing disciples and teaching them to live according to the values of Jesus is part of the mission, then ministry includes everything we do in order to help the people around us to experience the claim that Jesus makes upon their lives. Ministry is what is happening when the mission of the church is actually incarnate in its people now and here. Nothing could be more important for Christians than that ministry actually *happen*!

It would be very easy for us to assume that ministry is the only order of service that God is really interested in. One of the reasons that we sometimes slip into this mistaken assumption is that every Christian person is included in the order of ministry.

There are no Christian people who do not have the responsibility of ministry. My friend, Bishop Bob Farr, says that if you are still breathing you have a ministry, because the ministry God intends for you is the reason God gives you breath. Calvin (the four-year-old Calvin and Hobbs comic strip character, not the reformer) said, "God has put each person here on earth to accomplish certain things before they die. Right now, I'm so far behind, I may live forever."
Protestants have, for centuries, referred to the idea that we are here for a God-given purpose has, using the phrase "priesthood of all believers." Each Christian is called by

Christ to take up her or his cross and follow Jesus as a disciple. Since a disciple is one who follows a master in order to constantly learn and share in the work of the master, we are all part of the order of ministry.

That means that persons who are serving in the orders of management and governance are still responsible to live their lives as an expression of ministry, just as are all those whose work they are equipping, coordinating and aligning. And indeed, Christians may serve in each and all of these orders of service at various times or even at the same time through different roles in their lives. Christians are not "governors, managers or ministers" they are disciples who sometimes do governance, sometimes management, and always ministry.

Ministry in Congregational Life

But what does ministry actually look like? **Everything your church does or empowers its people to do is (or should be) ministry.** Ministry is everything that happens because of the mission of the church. Whether it is the work of a group or a single individual, if your people do something in order to express the mission of the congregation, it is ministry. And the ministry of your church happens both within and away from the church. Actually, most of the ministry of the church occurs when the people are dispersed and not when they are gathered as the church. If a church were living in perfect obedience to Christ, of course, it would not be doing anything for any other purpose than to fulfill the portion of the mission of Jesus assigned to them. Perfection is something to strive for, but it is rarely attained!

> *It would be very easy for us to assume that ministry is the only order of service that God is interested in. One of the reasons that we sometimes slip into this mistaken assumption is that every Christian person is included in the order of ministry.*

When Frank comes down to the sanctuary early on Sunday morning to make sure the heat is on, the hymnals are all in the racks, and the bulletins are folded, he is doing ministry. When Judy stops on her way home from work once a week to tend the flowerpots at the entrance to the church, she is doing ministry. When Gordon studies his Bible each morning making notes to teach the Bible study he leads on Wednesday noon, he is doing ministry.

But that hardly begins to touch the extent of ministry. When Alfred calls his short list of widows and widowers each day to make sure they are doing well and have what they need, he is doing ministry. When Melissa takes a deep prayerful breath before reacting to the bad behavior of the 5th grade boy in her public-school classroom she is doing ministry. When Alice volunteers at the local boys and girls club she is doing ministry.

When the choirs sing, when the breakfast is cooked for the annual family retreat, when the treasurer of the women's fellowship sends off their check for the fresh water project in Africa, when the peace with justice group lobbies the legislature for immigration reform, when the Habitat for Humanity group hands over the keys to the family with whom they have become friends as well as neighbors, they are all doing ministry.

When the AA group gathers in the church basement on Wednesday morning at 6:30, when Diana slips into the church's community garden to glean a few potatoes and beans, when Chair-of-Trustees Bob sacrifices the profit in his cabinet business to provide health insurance to his eight employees, when the OB nurse in the local hospital hands a new mother the handmade layette provided by the knitting group, ministry is happening.

And even this is not an exhaustive list! (Don't worry, I'm done listing - for now.) The real list is almost infinite. You must comprehend, as a church leader, that every activity and act of the disciples of your congregation that serves to embody the purpose of Jesus for your congregation is ministry. This is where the mission of Jesus is incarnate through the church. Even if your congregation has only 30 people I defy you to catalogue the potential impact of the ministry of your church through those 30 people when they understand their lives to **be** ministry.

> *You must comprehend, as a church leader, that every activity and act of the disciples of your congregation that serves to embody the purpose of Jesus for your congregation is ministry.*

When you understand ministry this way, then it is obvious that every Christian is a minister. And the ministry of every Christian is a responsibility that belongs to each one of us twenty-four-seven. It most certainly is NOT confined to what we do at church.

Every Christian is to strive to discern and to accept the ministry that Jesus prepared for him or her in particular. This means attending to the gifts and abilities that God has given you, and to the needs of the church and community in which God has placed you. Faithful ministry is what happens when you give the best that you have to give to the places where it will do the most good in addressing the needs of the neighbors that are actually before you. Before one can serve in a leadership role, one must be in ministry. And one never ceases the practice of discerning in order to remain in this process of following and serving as a disciple of Jesus.

The practice of ministry, which is the calling of every Christian, is not the focus of this book. *But you must understand that governance and management, which are the focus of this book, will have no relevance at all if the congregation being governed and managed does not understand and claim the practice of the ministry of all Christians.* In a congregation, ministry is the only thing worthy of being governed and managed.

Congregations that thrive build a culture in which every person understands that being a Christian means having a ministry.

The Order of Management

If there are two people attempting to work together in order to accomplish a common task, then there must be management. One of them must at least ask the other, "Which part do you want to do?"

Management is the work of leadership that must be done in order coordinate the work of a group of people to fulfill the responsibility that they share.

You will notice that, unlike the term *ministry*, the term *management* has no specifically religious or spiritual connotation. That's OK. Any group of people that want to work together to accomplish something will need to utilize management in order to coordinate the work. There are many ways to manage a group of people. Some are better for some kinds of tasks and some for others. Some good management models include: coaching, community organizing, foreman, project management and so on. There are also models of management that may succeed in getting something done, but are evil by nature: slavery, intimidation, demagoguery, despotism, shaming and so on.

Management models in the church must operate in ways that are consistent with the values of Jesus. Christian leaders should lead the way Jesus did. ***The people who perform management in the church must respect the dignity that is accorded a child of God (which includes, by definition, everyone).*** If you will keep that guiding principle in the foreground, it may help keep you on the right track.

Management is something we have all experienced (both as those whom others attempt to manage, and as those who try to manage others!). But what does it actually look like in the vital congregation? Who are the managers and what do they do?

Management in Congregational Life

In our good old Protestant congregations there are two titles that are often assigned to persons expected to do management among us, committee chair and staff person. Both of these positions in church organizations almost always imply that a group of people is being led to accomplish some shared responsibility. These days, sadly, all too often persons in these positions are actually expected to just do the ministry. They have become responsible not to manage a ministry, but to perform a ministry.

Think about the awful consequence of this development. If you have to be elected or hired in order to perform a ministry, then all those other Christians who have not been hired or elected must not be ministers. Many people who pretty regularly attend worship actually unconsciously believe this to be true. They think the ministers are those people up front, especially the ones who are paid. This is not how churches were meant to function.

> *If there are even just two people attempting to work together in order to accomplish a common task, then there must be management. One of them must at least ask the other, "Which part do you want to do?"*

Every time someone finds that it is his or her responsibility to try to get a group of people to do various parts of an effort with a relatively unified purpose, that person is serving as a manager. Management is what committee chairpersons and staff members are intended to do.

When Jane rises for the announcements time in worship to state that anyone interested in helping plan the family retreat should meet with her following worship, she is serving as a manager. When Bill sends an email to his list of gardeners indicating that he wants volunteers for the yard cleanup day next Saturday, he is serving as a manager. When Ellen prepares an outline of the actions and events that will constitute this year's stewardship campaign for the Finance Committee, she is serving as a manager.

One of the natural laws of human groups is that if something is happening, and if there is a group of people working together to make it happen, then someone is serving as a leader in the group by doing management. In many of the things that our congregations do, no one has been elected or identified in any formal way to "be the manager." But if you pay attention you will find that someone has "stepped up" to fill a leadership vacuum and serve as the manager.

Thriving congregations are very intentional about identifying the people who are responsible for managing their ministry groups. They select people with gifts and skills appropriate to coordinating a group of people. They train and equip them for the specific responsibilities assigned to them. They entrust to them ministries that motivate them and in which they feel a personal commitment. They clearly identify both the managers and the ministries for which they are responsible so that people in the congregation can find the ministry opportunities they are seeking.

There is a very unhelpful distinction being made in most churches between *staff* and *volunteers*. Of course, there is some meaning to this distinction: some people get paid something to fulfill their leadership responsibilities, and some people volunteer to do whatever they are doing in their congregation.

However, the much more important distinction is not whether people are being paid or not, but whether they are functioning in a responsibility for direct ministry, or a responsibility for managing a ministry. Your congregation must learn to treat those who manage ministries the same whether they are paid or not. We strongly recommend calling everyone who manages a ministry a *staff person* whether that position is paid or volunteer.

The Order of Governance

Whenever people are working together to accomplish a mission you can be sure that at some point they must have had a conversation that began something like, "So what should we do and why would we bother?" There can't be any mission, any purpose, if there has not been a discernment process by which someone identified and articulated what that purpose is. And if a purpose has been articulated and it is bigger than something that can be accomplished by just a handful of people, then there must also have been some kind of conversation about the question, "And how shall we go about doing it?"

Governance is the work of leadership that must be done in order to discover and articulate a mission and vision that will inspire people into service and to organize a strategy by which those inspired people may fulfill the mission.

Governance is another word that is used in all kinds of groups of people, not just by Christian groups. But Christians face a more complicated task in doing governance than do other groups. Those doing governance outside our Christian communities can ask one of two relatively simple questions in order to focus their work. They may ask, "What do I want to accomplish, and how can I inspire (or coerce) others into joining me in accomplishing it?" Or, they may ask a group of people, "What do we want to accomplish together, and how shall we do it?"

> *Whenever people are working together to accomplish a mission you can be sure that at some point they must have had a conversation that began something like, "So what should we do and why would we bother?"*

Christian congregations require governance that asks different questions, "What is the purpose for which Christ has called us? How will we find and engage with those whom he is calling us to invite into the life of discipleship? What is the transformation of the world we will incarnate together?"

Now we may be getting into new territory for you. Many of our congregations do not "do" governance for the simple reason that they assume it has already been done and that all we need to do is management and ministry. We came by this assumption honestly.

We have been doing church without asking why or what or with whom or how for a long time. Most of our congregations function on the assumption that everyone already knows what Christ is asking us to do (or at least what he wants us to not do).

It was most definitely enough for my parents' generation to know that they should teach Sunday school, go to worship, participate in their fellowship group, sing from the approved hymnal, serve on a committee when asked and tithe to their church. They did not *believe* that this would please God and fulfill their calling as Christians - they *knew* it would. They knew it the way a fish knows how to swim.

All that is gone. Even I am not old enough to remember a time when our assumption was true that everyone knew "why" and "what." Today, even our brothers and sisters who do Sunday school, attend worship, participate in a fellowship group, sing the accustomed music and support their church financially, argue with one another about whether that pleases God and fulfills their calling as Christians. These arguments upset us.

But the majority of people in our culture - those who do not do any of our churchy things - do not even have the question anymore. They watch the Sunday morning news shows or play their weekly round of golf or deliver their kids to the soccer tournament. And if a friend of theirs reports at coffee break on Monday morning that he or she went to church yesterday, they are mostly are just flummoxed. What is more, if they did care about their churchy friend enough to ask why he would want to do that, the odds are that the churchy friend could not provide and answer that would be compelling to anyone else standing around the coffee urn. (This is essential for you to understand.)

Governance is the leadership activity that discerns and articulates an inspiring God-given mission and the broad methods of ministry that the congregation will use to embody that mission in their place and time – the "why" and the "what" of being Christians. This has become the essential work of leadership in vital congregations, and it is often precisely the missing piece in congregations that are sliding into oblivion.

Governance in Congregational Life

It is very difficult to tell a story that captures what the work of governance looks like in our ordinary congregations. This is because the vast majority of our congregations do not regularly do anything intentional in the area of discerning and articulating their core purpose. There is very little attention paid to the question of how we will incarnate that mission in our actions. Indeed, we hardly ever ask whether what we are currently doing is serving our mission or not.

In congregations that are relatively lively, it is often the pastor who has stepped up to discern and articulate the mission and method of the congregation. In new congregations it is almost always the founding pastor who has done this, since

It was most definitely enough for my parents' generation to know that they should teach Sunday school, go to worship, participate in their fellowship group, sing from the approved hymnal, serve on a committee when asked and tithe to their church.

that is the first person there and everyone else is gathered around the vision that the founding pastor has been sharing. In any congregation, if there is a strong sense of purpose, it is essential that the pastor share in that sense of purpose. However, to see the work of governance as only or even primarily the pastor's responsibility is a grave error.

Truly vital congregations "do church" in ways that are intentionally designed to keep the core questions of governance in the foreground of their life together. What is the purpose for which Christ created our congregation? Who are the people to whom we have been sent? What are the kinds of ministries through which we intend to fulfill that purpose with those people? The most fundamental goal of this book is to help your congregation *organize* to enhance its ability to do the work of governance.

The table on page 97 summarizes the orders of ministry: Governance, Management and Ministry.

In the rest of the book we will be looking at how to organize a congregation in order to increase the ministry of all Christians, improve its ability to manage ministries for fruitfulness, and keep the mission of Christ at the center of its life and ministry together.

Table 1

	GOVERNANCE	MANAGEMENT	MINISTRY
PURPOSE	To discern and articulate the core purpose (mission), values, boundaries and goals of the congregation.	To align and coordinate the ministries of the congregation in order to fulfill the core purpose and goals of the congregation in ways consistent with its values and boundaries.	To express and incarnate the mission and purpose of the congregation in the lives of the people of the congregation and those to whom they are sent.
PROCESSES	Town Hall meetings, focus groups, prayer, holy conferencing, research, study.	Leadership of specific ministries intended to fulfill the mission of the congregation. Coordinate and align the various ministries so that they remain focused and faithful in mission.	Individual people working on their own and in ministry teams to express their unique gifts and interests in ways that support and extend the ministry of God through their church in all the places where they live and work.
STRUCTURE OR POSTIION	Church Council or Board	Pastor, paid staff, volunteer staff (ministry team leaders)	Every believer, church member, disciple.
ACCOUNTABILITY	To the mission God has for the congregation	To the Church Council or Board and to the mission	To the management of the congregation and to the mission.

Study Questions

1. How many ways can you list here that the people of your congregation are embodying the mission of Jesus in their lives?

2. Can the people in your congregation express what they understand their ministries to be? If not, how could your congregation do a better job of helping them to see themselves as ministers of the mission of Jesus?

3. How good is your congregation at specifically identifying those who are managers of the various team ministries of your congregation? Are there clear descriptions of responsibilities, authorities and accountabilities for them?

4. What official group or person in your congregation is responsible for governance (discerning and articulating the mission, vision and values of your congregation)? What processes do they use to accomplish that work?

Chapter Five
An Empowering Organization

What we want is a way to organize that makes it easier for our congregation to keep responsibility, authority and accountability aligned. It is also important that our structure help us to sustain the values and purpose of Jesus in the things we do and the way we do them. We want an organizational structure that helps every person in our congregation be encouraged and equipped to be in ministry, and to come to believe that ministry is the basic job description of every Christian.

We want a structure that helps us to practice the management of our ministries in a way that empowers the gifts of our people and helps them work together to fulfill the purpose Christ has ordained for us. And we want a structure that keeps us all attentive to the core missional questions of our congregation. What is our God-given purpose?

We need fewer experts and more experiments.

Who are the people to whom God is sending us? And what are the ministries that will fulfill that purpose?

It is crucial that we keep those questions of mission, neighbor and ministry at the center of our attention and effort. There was a time when the culture around us constantly affirmed the place of the church in society. Everywhere we went, the purpose of the church was assumed and affirmed. "Blue laws" prevented competing with church activities on Sundays and Wednesday evenings. Merchants gave pastors special discounts. People who didn't go to church generally felt guilty

101

about not going to church. We could go on, but you already know that cultural support of the church can no longer be assumed.

Some of us, myself included, think it has been bad for our faith that we have relied on the culture to support the church. Some of us believe that we are now at a place where, once again, the church is being called to be a counter-cultural community. Regardless of whether or not we like this new context for ministry, it is time for the church to "get over it" and "get on with it."

The way our congregations are structured was designed in, and for, that other time. It is not working in the times in which we find ourselves. We need a different way of ordering our life together so that we can address the demands of the mission field where we live now.

What follows is a description of core principles and of some specific practices that will help your congregation order its life in a way that is better able to make it fruitful in mission today. This is probably not the only way. If you and your fellow congregational leaders have some better ideas about how to be faithful and fruitful in mission, go for it. We need fewer experts and more experiments. But if you're just feeling stuck and frustrated by the processes and practices that you are accustomed to, what follows has been tried and it has proven helpful in liberating ministry, improving management, and implementing faithful governance that keeps a congregation centered in its mission.

Two Guiding Principles for Structures that Empower Ministry

Over the past thirty years church leaders from across the spectrum of traditions have struggled with the sense that things weren't working well anymore. Some of them began looking for signs of something that was working. They found a couple of common themes in the ways that vital congregations were organized. Almost without exception, vital congregations are organized in ways that are *flat* and *simple*. Indeed, these have been characteristic of powerful movements throughout history.

Keep it flat

A flat organizational structure is one in which there are very few steps from the bottom to the top or, more accurately, from the edge to the middle.

Figure A represents something like a standard model for United Methodist congregations, but it is very similar to the standard pattern for most mainline protestant congregations.

Your church may put different names to the boxes - but the boxes are usually there and arranged pretty much this way. There is an annual or all-church meeting where what are considered to be major issues will be decided by the whole congregation through debate and voting. Very democratic.

Figure A: Tall Structure

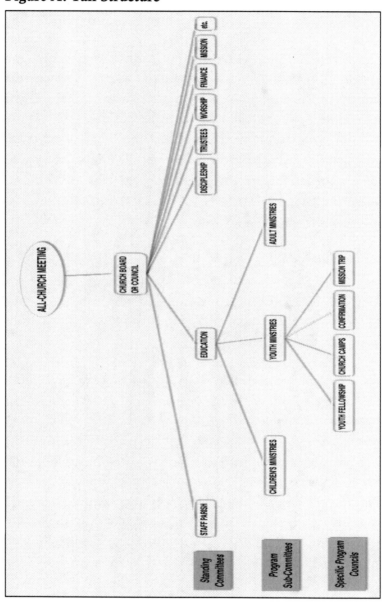

In most of our old-line denominations, everyone in all the boxes except the ones on the top and bottom of the chart are elected to these committees and councils. At each layer every committee may have one or more branches. I have only expanded one committee at each level in order to keep the illustration somewhat simple. Your congregation may have different committees from these, but the complexity of a multi-layered committee structure like this will be familiar to you.

This is not a flat structure. Suppose the person who is leading the youth mission trip (see it way down there at the bottom of the chart) believes they should discontinue the annual car wash that has been

> *Even if you don't actually have many committees anymore, if your official structure calls for them, then any innovative or significant idea will be blocked by the process that the structure demands (but does not practice except when there is innovation).*

used to fund the trip and instead fund it by selling "shares" in the mission. In this structure, that idea would first have to be approved by the Youth Ministries Council (step 1). The Youth Council chairperson would then take that idea to the Education Committee where it would be discussed and approved, disapproved or changed (step 2).

Once it passed the Education Committee it would then go to the Church Board or Council (step 3). That could be the end of it, but more likely the Church Council would ask that the idea be considered by the Finance and Mission Committees, whose representatives on the council expressed concerns about competing fund raising and mission activities (step 4 and maybe 5?). In this situation it would probably not go to an all-church meeting, but suppose the question was whether the youth ministry should begin a weekly youth worship experience on Sunday mornings. Such a proposal would probably require all the above steps plus an all-church meeting.

Many of your congregations no longer have this many layers in practice. You have been unable to fill all those positions for many years and just ignore most of the structure that exists on paper. I once served a congregation with a structure much like that in *Figure A* that had held only one Administrative Council meeting in the year before I came and there were no minutes of that meeting. All the real decisions were made at the Monday night Bible Study (to which no one was elected, and the pastor was not invited).

> *A flat organizational structure is one in which there are very few steps from the bottom to the top or, more accurately, from the edge to the middle.*

However, even if you don't have all the committees of your official structure, if your structure calls for them, then any innovative or significant idea will be blocked by the process that the structure demands (but does not practice except when there is innovation). All it takes is one fearful person to say, "We didn't follow the proper procedure," to stop anything we haven't done before.

In fact, in "tall structures" like **Figure A,** more things are prevented passively than are ever voted down. Innovative ideas just die of exhaustion trying to get a definitive answer.

In a flat organizational structure, we try do everything we can to limit the number of steps from the edge to the center. There are many reasons for us to do this.

- As we already know, most congregations simply do not have enough people to fill all the slots in their structure. The structure to which they are accustomed was developed when there were many more members in their churches, and many of those people had more volunteer time to give to church business. Now your willing servants end up serving on multiple committees. Often attendance at these meetings is intermittent at best. A flat structure dramatically reduces the number of committees and elected positions. Capable leaders can (and should) serve on just one committee each. They will make the time to be present because the issues they deal with will be significant and worthy of their time.

- Your best and boldest leaders, especially the new ones, are constantly frustrated by the amount of process and time involved in simply getting a "yes" or "no" to any novel proposal. They will often find that decisions regarding their responsibilities are made at meetings they were not invited to attend. The decisions made at those meetings are frequently based on incomplete or inaccurate information. Even when the information is accurate, decisions are seldom timely. A flat structure allows quick access to decisions made by people who are informed about the proposal and accessible to the people making the proposal. Even when the answer is no, at least the person being turned down is face to face with the person giving the answer.

- However, the most important reason to flatten your structure is that your "edge" is closer to your changing mission field than your "center." In a changing environment the center needs to be as immediately connected to the edge as possible. This will help increase the fruitfulness of the decisions made at the center because they will be more appropriate to the realities of your mission field. In an era when most people in our mission field see the church as irrelevant, we need to move our congregational decision-making closer to the edge - because that is where the mission exists.

In many of our congregations, decision-making is a little bit like having a committee in the back seat of the bus making all the decisions about whether to speed up or slow down, turn right or turn left, or hit the brakes. The bus driver (who is actually looking out the windshield!) is not allowed to make those decisions without first checking with the committee in the back. A flat structure moves those kinds of immediate decisions up to the person actually holding the wheel and looking out the windshield. Of course, the people in the back of the bus should absolutely still have a say about where they are going!

Figure B) A Flat Structure

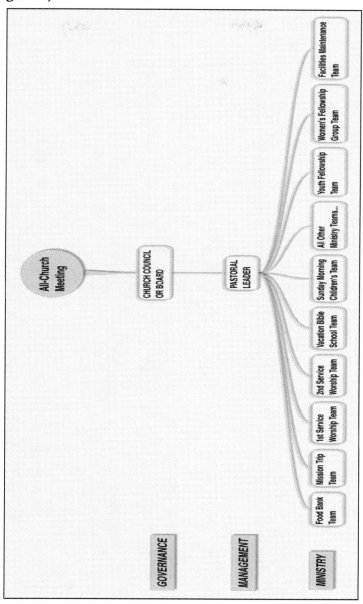

Figure B illustrates a flat structure. In Figure B you will notice that the pastoral leader is accountable to the church council, which is elected by the church to lead the congregation. In this position the pastor is responsible for coordinating and aligning all the various ministries of the congregation in order to fulfill their shared intention.

The ministries are all made up of teams of people who have made a personal commitment to do the ministries in which they are involved. *Ministry teams are not elected. Members of ministry teams self-select themselves through personal and particular interest in the ministry.* The whole church elects the Church Council to discern and articulate their purpose and to work with the pastor and other leaders to determine the basic methods of ministry they will employ to fulfill the mission.

> *Having a simple structure means that your church culture makes it simple for someone to become a confident and competent participant in the congregation.*

A flat structure makes it possible for someone who has responsibility for a ministry to make a single phone call to get a yes or no answer to any question they have regarding the performance of that ministry. A flat structure also means that your ministry managers are accountable to a single person for the ministry responsibility they bear.

As you can see, any ministry team leader can go directly to the pastor to receive a decision on almost any ministry idea (one step). The pastor can access the wisdom and guidance of the Council in situations where the needed decision is significant enough to warrant that consultation (two steps). This structure places every ministry leader no more than three steps from even a decision significant enough to require an all-church vote.

People sometimes think this is too much power, or too much burden, for a pastor to bear. But they bear it already, just without any authority to match their responsibility.

Keep it Simple

At first glance, flat and simple look like the same thing. On a diagram they are. As you can see, the flat structure is much simpler than the tall structure. If the congregation with the tall structure doubles the number of ministries, it will add more committees with more sub-branches for programs. The networks and layers will increase with size. The congregation with the flat structure will just add more Ministry Teams connected through the pastor, and no new layers are created. Simple.

Keeping a structure simple goes beyond keeping it flat, however. Those structure diagrams do not reflect things like policy manuals, unwritten policies, "the way we've always done it" and a myriad of other complexities that can encumber even a flat structure.

> *Ministry teams are not elected, they self-select themselves out of a personal particular interest in the ministry.*

Having a simple structure means that your church culture makes it simple for someone to become a confident and competent participant in the congregation. A simple structure *actually functions according to the organizational diagram,* whatever it is.

In a church with a simple structure it is easy for people to know the answers to questions like these:

* Who do I ask for permission to do something in or on behalf of the church? (How does something become a ministry of the church?)
* What kinds of activities are approved and supported in this church, and what kinds of activities are prohibited? (What are our behavioral boundaries?)
* What do we expect of those who desire to lead a ministry here? (What are our expectations of one another?)
* How do I grow as a faithful member of this community of faith? (How do I become what you mean when you call someone a disciple)?

Keeping a structure simple goes beyond keeping it flat, however. Those structure diagrams do not reflect things like policy manuals, unwritten policies, "the way we've always done it" and a myriad of other complexities that can encumber even a flat structure.

It is easy for us to sketch out a flat structure for our church. It is much harder for long-time church people (like most of you reading this) to keep the church simple. We already know the answers to all the questions above so well that we probably can't even answer them. It's like trying to give someone directions to somewhere you have driven every day of your life. You can't even remember what the landmarks are anymore.

We have learned all those things over a very long period of time and the answers are in our very bones. This is why visiting church for the first time is a lot like going to someone else's family reunion. The whole experience is filled with conversations and activities that seem to make sense to everyone else, but we just know that we are missing something they all "get."

> *It takes constant effort to help our people to understand that they are not entitled to have their expectations met by everyone else in the community unless those expectations have been agreed upon and explicitly shared.*

Congregations that are empowering learn that they need to be able to "use their words" to answer those questions. Authority to make decisions or to establish behavioral boundaries and expectations should be simple and explicit. Everyone in your congregation should easily be able to answer questions like those above while standing in line for coffee after worship.

For example, if we say that new ministry programs must be approved by the church council - that would be simple. (Let me add that I would not recommend that policy!) But in many churches, even after the Church Council has approved something, there will be open and ongoing debate about whether we should allow it. And there are often people in the congregation who will not hesitate to tell other people that something should not be happening (never mind that the official processes of the congregation have approved it).

For us crusty old-timers, that kind of behavior is just background noise, but it is deadly for new people who think they have gone through the appropriate process and then find themselves confronted by someone with unwritten rules or their own divergent opinion. In a simple structure (and a vital congregation), it will not be enough to be clear about who can allow or deny a request, it must also be clear who does NOT have that authority.

One of the fundamental convictions of simple congregations is that if something is not prohibited through the explicit processes, then it is allowed. It takes constant effort to help people understand that everyone is not entitled to have their expectations met by everyone else in the community unless those expectations have been agreed upon and explicitly adopted by the community. If everyone is actually supposed to dress up for Sunday service, then the whole church must say so, for heaven sake. Don't wait until someone comes to church in shorts and then criticize them.

Do I need to say that simple congregations get choosy about their expectations? Do you really care if everyone's hairdo meets a standard? A simple congregation will keep the number of rules and boundaries down to a number that can be easily explained and quickly learned. These rules and boundaries will be about things that matter to everyone in the church. *Ideally, they will be about things that matter to Jesus.*

One way to do this is to use "marker expectations." When I visited Cedar Ridge Community Church in Maryland they had a thing they called "seven minutes of Cedar Ridge." At the end of worship, they invited newcomers who wanted to know more about their church to come up to the front row for a seven-minute presentation about Cedar Ridge Community Church. They also promised you a nice little gift.

About fifteen people joined in the front row that day after church to hear what they had to say. The associate pastor who gave the talk started out with something like this, "Cedar Ridge is a church that believes in radical grace and so welcomes everyone. That means that, if you make this your spiritual home, you will see all kinds of people here; many races, gay and lesbian couples, people with tattoos and body piercings – you just never know! We believe that none of us is perfect and all of us are on a journey and that God is with all of us right where we are."

After the talk I spent a bit of time with the pastor who led it. "Gee," I said, "I'm surprised that practically the first thing you say is that gay and lesbian people are welcome here. Seems like some people might not listen to another thing you say!"

> To be simple, your congregation needs to come to some clarity about what is essential to you together, and then everything else will be "think and let think."

His answer was brilliant and very insightful. "Why would we want someone to waste six weeks or six months going to church here only to storm out when they one day learn that we are a grace-based community where all kinds of people are welcome and included?" For Cedar Ridge Community Church, the sexual identity issue was a marker value. At that time (early 2000s) if you said that about your church it said a whole lot about many other things you might expect or not expect there.

As you think about making your church more simple, talk together about what is really important to your people. Ask them what they believe is really important to God. Then focus on that core of values and practices and share them and stand on them. Leave the other stuff, whatever it may be, behind. As John Wesley put it so simply, "In essentials, let us agree, in all else let it be think and let think." To be simple, your congregation needs to come to some clarity about what is essential to you together, and then everything else will be "think and let think."

Simple congregations also have a very small number of categories into which they put their people.

> *"All the old fashions are now obsolete. Words like Jewish and non-Jewish, religious and irreligious, insider and outsider, uncivilized and uncouth, slave and free, mean nothing. From now on everyone is defined by Christ, everyone is included in Christ." (Colossians 3:11 The Message)*

My denomination has at least the following confusing categories of people: several categories of elders (retired, active, on leave, extension, honorably located, and more), several categories of deacons, deaconesses, licensed local pastors, lay pastors, baptized members, professing members, charter members, associate members, affiliate members, and constituents. While they were not created as a way to honor some and dismiss others, it seems to be the way of human beings to see them that way. Your church may have a similar reality.

Simple congregations tend to have fewer categories of people, while at the same time they multiply the significance of the diversity of the individuals in the congregation! They decrease the number of *categories* of people by having no more than two or three different categories. These very few categories tend to define responsibilities, not rights or value (board member, member, everyone else).

On the other hand, they increase the *diversity* of people by seeing each and every person as a unique individual with particular and precious gifts and interests. They further see these people as having been called into the Body of Christ for their equally particular and precious diverse roles in fulfilling the purpose of God for the congregation.

In a simple congregation everyone has the same status, that of a disciple, and each and every disciple has his or her own particular calling that contributes to the mission of the whole.

Fruitful congregations are flat and simple. If your church has been around for more than a few years you can be almost certain it has become "tall" and "complicated." Even if you have just one committee, you should ask how much someone has to know before he or she can really take his or her place among you. If you think someone who has been coming to your church for three or four years doesn't yet have enough experience with you to serve in leadership, then you are a complicated church. If someone who has been coming to worship with you for three months doesn't know what you mean by words like *Christian*, *disciple* or *member* you are a complicated church.

If your church is complicated, it will take some very intentional conversations to rediscover the core of the purpose that Jesus has for you. The next section of the book commends a structure to you that is designed to nurture those conversations.

1. Sketch out the structure of your congregation from your own memory and knowledge. Ask another leader in your congregation to do the same. Ask a non-leader in your congregation to do the same.

   a. Do you all have the same answer?

   b. Does this sketch actually represent the way decisions are made? (If the structure makes a decision, can that decision be reversed by "influencers" within the congregation?)

   c. Would you say your structure is tall or flat?

2. Is it easy for new people to understand how decisions are made in your congregation?

   a. Can new ideas get a real yes or no answer in less than a month?

   b. Can you identify the person in your congregation who has the responsibility and authority to align and coordinate the ministries of the congregation?

   c. Would you say your congregation is simple or complicated?

3. What are the core expectations and values of your congregation?

   a. Who discerns and articulates these core values?

   b. Are they listed, taught in an orientation class, or otherwise explicitly shared in the congregation?

   c. Do new people in your congregation "trip over" unwritten rules and expectations as they seek to become part of you?

   d. Can you identify some "unwritten rules" that seem to be operating in your congregation?

Chapter Six
Empowering Leaders

Nothing in your organization will work unless you get the right people in the right places. How do you do that? Before we look at the structural pieces that make up a fruitful congregation, we should think about how you would find the right people to fill each of those structures.

The process used to populate your structure with fruitful and faithful leaders will be a *call process*.

Our accustomed way of selecting leaders is a *recruiting process*. We start with a box on our chart to fill and assume that we just keep·trying until we find someone to fill it. As we all know, this often ends up being someone who says, "If no one else will do it, I guess I could."

We recruit people instead of call people into leadership because we believe deeply that we must keep doing what we are already doing. If we have had an Annual Labor Day BBQ to raise funds for the mission fund, we are absolutely convinced that our mission fund would disappear if we did not have an Annual Labor Day BBQ. We know this even if everyone in our town under fifty no longer eats meat and leaves town on Labor Day, and if all the money raised is coming from the same people who are putting on the BBQ. So, we must fill the box "Chairperson for the Annual Labor Day BBQ" no matter how much arm-twisting is required.

We will continue to do this recruiting even when people always refuse to do the job a second time. We will continue to do this recruiting even when people quit the church as a result of their experience of doing the job. *(You do know Jesus funded his mission without ever holding the Labor Day BBQ – right?)*

We also recruit, instead of call, people into leadership and ministry because we believe deeply that there are many things God demands of us that nobody would ever want to do.

When I was a young pastor I hated recruiting teachers for children's Sunday school. I like to teach adult classes. That's my calling. I like kids, but I don't really like teaching Sunday school, and when I say, "don't really like," I mean I would prefer major dental surgery (at least they anesthetize you for that). So, when I recruited Sunday school teachers, I always felt like I was asking people to do something that they would really rather not do.

You can imagine the process. "Hi, Sandy," I would say, "I'm calling because Trudy's husband got transferred and they had to move and so we really don't have anyone to teach the pre-school Sunday School class. I know it's a lot to ask, (desperation in my voice!) but I don't suppose you'd be willing to take it on, would you? There really isn't anyone else who could do it."

> *We recruit people instead of call people into leadership because we believe deeply that we must keep doing what we are already doing.*

My error was assuming that Sandy (and for that matter everyone else) felt the same about teaching children's Sunday School as I do, which was a ridiculous assumption on my part. I was also convinced that I would be in trouble with my church if I didn't keep all their programs going, which is not such a ridiculous assumption for a pastor. Even worse, Sandy was being told by of the style of my approach that this was an unpleasant job, and that if she consented to do it we would all know that it would be a sacrifice not a calling. The best she could hope for from us was that she might be honored at some point.

To get out of the recruiting mode we will need to abandon convictions and assumptions like these:
- We must do what has always been done.
- God demands that we all do stuff we hate doing.
- Everyone hates doing the same things I hate doing and everyone wants to do the same stuff I want to do.
- Never ask why we have to do this.

Let's think about the convictions that support a call system.

Convictions Behind A Call Process

If God wants your church to do it, God will provide the leaders and doers to make it happen.

When we follow a call process, we assume that God is keeping track of two things at the same time – assigning a responsibility to our congregation and calling the people who will provide for that particular responsibility. We believe that God does not make mistakes in this regard (though we might). God is actually capable of doing more than one thing at the same time. A lot more.

This means that there are two sides to a call process, both of which must be attended to if we are going to call someone to a leadership position. On one side is the discernment of the church affirming that God assigns a particular responsibility to be done and that a particular person has been called by God to do it; and on the other side is a person with the inner conviction that God is calling him or her to do this job.

This all sounds very spiritual and theological and hard to dispute – until there is some job we think needs to be done, but nobody is feeling a personal sense of calling to do it. When that happens, we generally assume that somebody needs to do it even if nobody is feeling called. This effect is most persistent when the job we think needs to be done is one that has "always been done." As a result, we use everyone up doing the things we have always done, whether anyone feels called to do them or not.

To be fruitful, we will need to be willing to allow some things to NOT be done because no one is recognizing a personal calling to do it. This brings us to the essential conviction that "no" is a holy answer and we need to tell people that.

The Holy Spirit is trustworthy to guide both those doing the calling and those being called.

When we are calling people into leadership responsibilities we trust that the Holy Spirit will actually guide us to call the right person to the right responsibility. This addresses the first side of the matter. We will also trust that the Holy Spirit will guide those we are calling. In fact, we will encourage those we are calling into leadership to trust the Holy Spirit to guide them in their response to our calling. We will only consider a calling legitimate when both sides have the same sense of the leading of The Spirit.

To be fruitful we need to be faithful in aligning an outward calling from the church with an inward calling of God.

Every person has abilities and passion that God intends to use to empower the church and to bless the world.

If this is true, then we will need to listen more deeply to one another. We must seek to discover what God has given us love and concern for.

If we could help people apply the innate God-given grace they possess to the place in life they most passionately care about, that would transform the world.

The Pharisees asked Jesus, "Who is my neighbor?" One way to understand the story he used to answer the question is that your neighbor is the person you notice. (Jesus ends the story with the question, "Who was neighbor to the man?") The Samaritan was the neighbor because he noticed the man and felt compassion. Those two facts of his experience were the calling that drove all the rest of the Good Samaritan's actions.

It is amazing how different people care about different things. If we could help people make a positive difference in things they actually care about, the results would be amazing.

Listening more deeply to others will help us to discover what gifts and skills they have been given. Most of us are keenly aware and proud of the stuff we have learned and the skills we have developed. But often it takes others to point out to us the beauty and grace that we bring without even noticing it because God created it in us. If we could help people begin to comprehend and express the innate gifts God has given them, well, that would be amazing too.

If we could help people apply the innate God-given grace they possess to the place in life they most passionately care about, that would transform the world.

To be fruitful we need to start calling people to fulfill their vocations, instead of recruiting them to do their chores.

Who carries out the Calling Process?

In any congregation there will be a variety of persons and groups who will be inviting (not to say coercing) people into specific responsibilities. In a really faithful and fruitful congregation, this call process will be the way that disciples become engaged in ministry no matter who is doing the calling.

A calling process works best when a specific ministry team in the congregation carries the responsibility of identifying, calling and equipping disciples for leadership and ministry.

Since making disciples for the transformation of the world is the core mission of the church, identifying, calling and equipping disciples in ministry is a very important core practice.

If your church has any kind of nominating body (in the UMC it is the committee on lay leadership and nominations), it should understand itself to be a *calling* committee.

The Practice of a Calling Process

The process described here works best with a group of people acting as a calling team.

A nominating committee or church council will use this process whenever they are nominating people for core leadership positions in the congregation. Any ministry team may also use it as it seeks to call others to share in its ministry. Even individuals who are building a ministry team can use the calling process to build their team.

There will be two sides to a call process, both of which must be fulfilled if we are going to commission someone to a leadership position. On the one side is the conviction of the church that God expects a particular job to be done and that a particular person is the best person to do it; and on the other side is a person with the inner conviction that God is calling him or her to do this job.

Describe the calling

You really can't decide who should be asked to do something until you know what it is you want them to do. The very first question you need to answer in a calling process is, "What is the responsibility we are asking someone to fulfill?"

Don't settle for something like, "Chair the annual mission trip." Your description of the responsibility should include:
- Information about who is to be served by this ministry, and
- What impact this ministry will have on the lives of the persons served.

You should include in the description of the responsibility details, like the dates when the responsibility begins and when it ends. You should make an honest estimate of the amount of time that a person might expect to spend in fulfillment of the responsibility.

Describe the authority granted and the boundaries established for this leader.

Next you will want to make clear what authority the person you are seeking will have to work with. Is there a budget, and if yes how much? If there is no budget, can the team do fund-raising on their own? What facilities and equipment are available to carry out this responsibility? Where is it expected to happen? For example, if the ministry is supposed to happen away from the church facilities, make sure that is clear. If it must happen at the church, make that clear as well.

Are there specific times or dates allowed, or is authority to set these delegated to the leader? For example, is it required that this ministry occur on Sunday morning? If so, it should be clear in the description.

Are there specific means required? Must all the music come from the hymnal? Are there safe sanctuary policies that must be adhered to? Make sure any limits regarding the strategies are explicit and clear.

> *A calling process works best when a specific ministry team in the congregation carries the responsibility of identifying, calling and equipping disciples for leadership and ministry.*

Can this leader call any persons they want to assist them? What are the minimum qualifications, if any, for the people they will call to help them with this responsibility? (For example, must they be members of the congregation, must they be Christians, must they pass a background check, and so on?)

Unless the ministry you are calling a leader to lead is already very successful, do not place more limits that you absolutely need to provide for the safety of those involved and the values of the congregation. Innovation is stifled by too many limits on your leaders. If you have not specified something in the calling description – the leader should be able to assume freedom is given.

Define the accountability.

What qualities, skills, practices, availability and gifts are desired or required in the person called to carry out this responsibility? For example, is membership in the church required? Does this person need to be regular in worship, a financial contributor, available for Tuesday morning staff meetings, pass a background check, competent with computer software, or demonstrate a significant commitment to a personal spiritual discipline?

Does this leader need to be able to recruit their own team or work with an existing team? Do you need someone who can speak before the congregation or will this position be more behind the scenes?

Is this position paid or volunteer? How much vacation or leave time is allowed and how is it to be arranged? Even volunteers need to know if they are supposed to get someone to cover their responsibility when they are sick or away.

To whom will this person be accountable? How will the outcomes of this ministry be evaluated? (Yes, even volunteer ministry leaders will have clear responsibility and accountability!)

Figure C is an example of a calling description for a church facilities manager from an actual church!

Figure C: **Example Calling Description – next page.**

An example of a Calling Description
Facilities Ministry Team Leader (FTL) *(unpaid staff position)*

All staff members of the Anywhere Community Church are in ministry. As such they are all expected to devote themselves to serve, to the best of their ability, as Christ would ask of them. Our staff members will endeavor to treat each person they encounter in the pursuit of their ministries as a child of God.

The Facilities Ministry Team Leader is a volunteer staff position.

The purpose of the FTL is to assure that the facilities and equipment of the congregation are maintained in the best possible condition to support its mission and vision. The FTL will maintain and manage a Facilities Ministry Team in assuring that the facilities and equipment of the congregation are clean, safe, and ready for all our approved activities, ministries, guests and visitors. Our goal is that everyone who enters our facility will feel welcome and safe. We want our facilities to provide an environment where people can encounter the grace of God. The FTM will also assure that facilities and equipment are insured according to current standard practice. The FTL will participate in the weekly staff meeting to coordinate facilities management with the other staff.

Performance of the role of the FTL is expected to require approximately 20 hours per week. Presence during worship times and weekly staff meetings is required. The FTL is entitled to a month of vacation each year, during which a substitute will be arranged with approval of the Pastor.

The FTL will serve in this calling as long as the FTL feels called to fulfill this ministry and the congregation's leaders feel that the ministry is being fulfilled consistent with the needs of our mission. Termination of the commitment to this calling may occur at the will of either the FTL or of the Pastor at any time.

The FTL will have spending authority for the Facilities Budget established annually by the Church Council. The FTL is expected to call a Facilities Team of members and friends of the church sufficient to support the responsibilities of the team. The FTL may also, when necessary, hire or contract for needed services beyond the capability of the team. If special maintenance or repairs are needed that extend beyond the budget available, the FTL will consult with the Pastor regarding how to proceed.

The FTL will be accountable to the Pastor. Evaluation of the FTL will be based on the following: evidence of commitment to the mission and values of the congregation, calling and nurturing a facilities team adequate to the responsibility, readiness of the facilities for the ministries and activities of the congregation, sustaining a quality working relationship with the staff team, and timely and efficient care for administrative duties (such as financial reporting, insurance information, and so on).

One of the most powerful things a congregation can do to begin a move toward vitality is to establish as core practices that:

- We will not ask anyone to serve in a leadership position that does not have a complete Ministry Description.
- We will not fill any leadership position with someone who does not acknowledge a sense of personal calling to the position.

Prioritize the callings of your congregation.

A common mistake of nominating committees is to deploy leaders in ways that are unfruitful for the mission of the congregation. To avoid this mistake, it is important that you discern which ministry positions are most important to fulfilling the mission and vision of God for your congregation.

Once you have calling descriptions for the most demanding ministry positions in your church, you should put them in order according to how essential they are to the mission and vision of the congregation.

List all the open ministry callings your calling team is being asked to fill. Ask each person on the calling committee to rank them in order of their importance to the mission and vision of the congregation. Then work through them as a group and reach a consensus regarding the order of significance.

When you begin calling leaders, always begin with the most significant positions and work your way through the list from there. Remember that significance, in this regard, has nothing to do with honor. What matters is which positions are most central to fulfilling the mission and vision of the congregation. It is really somewhat tragic to have asked someone to fulfill a calling, to have received an affirmation, and then begin working on another calling only to realize that he or she should really have been called there.

Discern candidates for a specific calling.

(I will describe how discernment works in a team process, but you can easily adapt it to calling others to work with you as a team leader.)

Having reviewed the calling description being discerned, enter into silent listening prayer and allow any names to come to mind that may

> *It is very important that you NOT invent assumed reasons that a person may say no.*

do so. Do not reject any of the names that come to mind during prayer. Instruct members of your calling team to report every name that comes to mind while in prayer, whether they consider it to be a good idea or not. Place these names on a flip chart or white board where everyone can see all the names.

Briefly discuss each person on the list. What do we know about his or her gifts? How have we experienced this person? Why do we imagine this name came to us in prayer? It is very important that you *NOT* invent assumed reasons that the person may say no. So often we say things like, "Well, Mary has that two-year-old who is really a handful and I doubt she would have time for this calling." Mary might be looking desperately for something meaningful to do 5 hours a week that does not involve someone saying, "Mommy!" in a whiney voice. Focus on the match between the perceived gifts and skills of the person and those required in the calling. Do not presume to answer for people. Let people say no (or yes!) for themselves.

Prioritize the listed names. (Have each person vote for his or her top three choices or use any other means you are familiar with to put the list of names in priority order for the call team.) Identify the top three nominees.

Extend the call.

For each particular calling identify one person on your call committee to act as the contact person for this call. Ideally this will be someone with familiarity with the demands of the calling. In some cases, you may choose someone who is familiar with the person you intend to call to the position.

A letter is sent to the first-choice person with the description of the call including:
- The calling description,
- Why this person is our choice for this position,
- That calling is a sacred trust requiring both the church's recognition of a call and the candidate, inner sense of calling, and
- That if accepting this calling requires letting go of a currently held responsibility in the church, we would be glad to relieve you of other callings if you feel more called to this one.

- That your contact will call you in a week to see what your answer is, and,
- That we trust your faithfulness in responding and that, since we are not aware of your other commitments or internal sense of call, we know that "no" may be a holy answer.

Your contact will phone the person a week after the letter was sent for his or her answer. *Do you have questions? Have you had an opportunity to pray about this? We want you to be serving in the place where your community's need and your passion intersect, so "no" may be a holy answer. Do you have an answer for us?* Whatever the answer, express gratitude and respect for the faithfulness of the person who has honestly and sincerely considered this calling. Make sure that he or she knows that the church is committed to helping all its disciples find the place God wants them in ministry. It is especially important that a negative response be affirmed.

In most cases a phone call is the best way to make this contact for a decision. The phone call is personal and allows for easy and human back and forth to really come to a clear understanding. A personal visit may be good but can make it quite difficult for the person being called to say no. Email is too impersonal. Conversation in public can be coercive!

Figure D: Example Call Letter –   *on next page*

Dear Susan,

I am writing to you on behalf of the calling committee of Anywhere Church. We have been prayerfully considering whom God may be calling to serve as the Facilities Ministry Team Leader for our congregation. We have agreed to extend an invitation to you as the person we feel is best equipped to fulfill this calling. The team is very familiar with the reliability of your leadership in previous callings in our church. You have demonstrated an ability to inspire others to cooperate in carrying out a variety of significant ministries such as the Mother's Day out and the family retreat. We have also noticed that you seem to have both interest in the physical spaces of our church facilities and knowledge of matters related to maintaining a welcoming environment. We believe you would be excellent in this position and that the fruitfulness of our overall mission would be enhanced by your service in this calling.

You will find the description of the calling included with this letter. We hope that you will spend the next week prayerfully considering this calling. Please feel free to discuss it with anyone you wish. If you want more detailed information about the calling, you may want to speak to John Smith who is just stepping down from this ministry after serving for three years. You can also call me with any questions you may have.

We know that this calling involves a significant commitment of time. We are not asking you to add this to the other commitments you have made to the congregation. We see your service in this ministry as more impactful than in the other positions you are currently filling in the congregation, and we would anticipate that accepting this calling may involve your resignation from some or all of your other church ministry commitments.

In about a week I will phone you to see if you have any further questions, or if you are ready to give us an answer. We understand that, though we see you as the right person to undertake this ministry, we are not familiar with the many other commitments and aspirations God has placed upon you. Because of that, we want to assure you that "no" is a holy answer. If you feel that you are not called to this responsibility at this time, we hope you will decline. Together we want to work with you to discern the calling that best matches your deepest gifts with the world's greatest needs.

Should you discern that this is indeed a calling from God in your life, we promise to support you with any training or other assistance you may need to perform this calling with excellence. We would be very excited to welcome you in leadership in this ministry.

Thank you in advance for your already faithful commitment to discipleship and to the mission of the church we love. Whatever your answer may be, we will continue to celebrate the relationship of common mission and fellowship we enjoy with you in the Body of Christ.

Yours in Christ,
Fred Jones.

If the answer is yes

Hooray! But please do not consider yourselves to have completed your work! You will certainly want to offer the person who has just accepted the calling whatever orientation, training, and support, is appropriate to the ministry. This is the point where a face to face visit is a great idea.

As this person works to fulfill the calling he has accepted, be sure to recognize signs of faithfulness and fruitfulness in the performance of this responsibility. And do not forget that the best accountability you can offer is for someone to regularly ask how it is going in the responsibility given. Is more support needed? Is the responsibility badly conceived and does it need to be reconsidered? It is much better to revise a ministry position description or to help people exit a calling themselves because they have discerned it is a bad fit, than to have them struggle with failure-in-place.

If the answer is no

Remember that you identified your top three choices for the position? If number one declines, extend the call to number two in the same way. If number two declines, extend the call to number three. *If your top three choices all decline do not fill the position*. This is the difficult, but crucial, commitment you must make if your call system is to work faithfully. If you have discerned and called your first three choices and they have all declined, you need to take that very seriously.

If your top three choices all decline, do not fill the position. This is the difficult, but crucial, commitment you must make if your call system is to work faithfully.

Have you created a calling description that is too demanding? Can it be broken into smaller pieces? You may be able to call others (or even your top three choices) to a revised call description that addresses their concerns. Be careful not to just revise it to a useless position, however!

Have you created a calling description that actually doesn't matter? Just because you have always had this position, or just because your council thinks it is important doesn't mean it is necessarily relevant anymore. Should you be looking at whether or not this position actually matters?

Would it be better to contract this responsibility out? Many congregations have discovered, for example, that they get better financial support by hiring a bookkeeping service to write the checks and do payroll. These services provide regular monthly reports to your management team, and none of your members is saddled with worrying about keeping the books. There are many tasks better done by an outside contractor.

Sometimes something has to stop happening for a while so that people can recognize its value. Allowing a ministry or regular event to stop happening for a season often allows someone to discover his or her real passion for that ministry. Ministries truly valuable to a congregation will not languish for long before someone discovers a calling to revive it, often in a better form than before.

Consequences of a serious commitment to a Calling Process

If you exercise this call system in your congregation you will be surprised by a number of things that develop.

- You will be surprised how ready and grateful people are to be invited to actually consider a calling.

- You will be surprised how many people say yes. In my experience about 80% of our first-choice people say yes to the calling. More than 90% of the time a calling is filled with one of our top three choices.

- You will be surprised how hard it is to decide to let something rest when nobody is experiencing a call to keep it going.

- You will be surprised at how well the church works even when you let some things that you thought were essential go because your top three choices all declined the calling.

- You will be surprised how frequently someone spontaneously steps up to volunteer out of a personal sense of commitment to do ministry in a position that you could not fill (and the job is not being done).

- You will be a bit surprised how often you really don't need to restart something that you considered essential.

- You will be surprised at how much more positive people feel about the leadership roles they serve in the church.

- You will be surprised at how much more seriously everyone takes their responsibilities and at how faithfully they perform in the ministries they take on.

Now, with our leadership calling process firmly in place, we are ready to talk about how to structure our leadership system for fruitfulness in mission.

Study Questions

1. How many official leadership positions does your congregation currently specify?

   a. How many of your leaders are currently holding more than one leadership position?

   b. How many of your official leadership positions are currently vacant?

   c. How many written ministry descriptions do you have currently? Do these include all the elements of a complete ministry description?

2. How would you feel about receiving the kind of ministry description and calling letter described in this chapter?

3. What seems most impractical about this calling system as you ponder implementing it in your congregation?

4. What seems most promising about this calling system as you consider implementing it in your congregation?

Chapter Seven
The Church Council

In a flat and simple congregation, the responsibility for **governance** will be carried by just one group. I will call this governing group the Church Council, but your governing body may be called the Church Council, the Church Board, the Board of Elders, The Session, or anything else you want. What matters is what this group does. It is important that only one group in the congregation bear this responsibility. In a fruitful congregation some group must have this function, but in most churches, no one actually does this work. It is not a coincidence that most churches are not thriving since the work of governance is essential for a congregation to remain vital in a changing mission environment.

Governance is the essential leadership responsibility to discern and articulate the mission, vision, values and boundaries of the congregation. While the pastor must be a mouthpiece and cheerleader for the mission, vision and values, the pastor is not the source of these motivating forces in the life of a congregation. And no one person can discern and articulate these God-given essentials alone.

> *Again, truly I tell you, if two of you agree on earth about anything you ask, it will be done for you by my Father in heaven. For where two or three are gathered in my name, I am there among them.*
>
> *(Matthew 18:19-20)*

> *Governance refers to the essential leadership responsibility to discern and articulate the mission, vision, values and boundaries - for the congregation.*

It is equally true that the whole congregation cannot be the group that articulates the mission, vision and values. If there are more than about fifteen people involved in this work, it will just end up being a kind of vague and abstract thing with no motivating force, or a laundry list of everyone's individual loyalties and desires that can never be fulfilled. This is why there must be, at the center of every congregation, a small group of people with the responsibility to discern a "who we are" and "what God wants of us."

The Church Council must be that group. Those who hold the vision must also hold the reins. The questions that drive their work are...

- *Who are we?* What are the gifts and resources available for ministry in our congregation? What do we care about? What are our shared passions? How do we comprehend the calling of God individually and as a body? What are we good at and what do we do poorly? What are our shared convictions?

- *Who is our neighbor?* Who is God sending us to engage with right now in order to bring them the good news and to invite them into the way of discipleship of Jesus Christ? (Matthew 28:19-20) To whom is God sending us right now in order that they might be healed, liberated, fed, and redeemed? (Luke 4:18-21, John 21:15-19)

- *What is our definition of a disciple?* What would it mean to me (and look like) to be a disciple in this congregation? What does a disciple believe and do?

The definition of your neighbor must be specific enough so that your disciples know who they are really called to build relationship with outside the church. It should take into account where your current people are in the normal course of their daily lives. Who are they seeing and interacting with on a daily basis (co-workers, physical neighbors, etc.). It should take into account who they know how to talk to and who they care about.

The definition of a disciple must be clear enough and specific enough to distinguish the disciples in your congregation from all those other nice folks with whom you share your daily lives. It should set a direction in the life of each person who desires to be a disciple in the manner characteristic of your community.

> *In our current missional context in America, to be a disciple is a counter-cultural way of living, but disciples are not to be so completely counter-cultural that they are isolated from their neighbors.*

Your definition of discipleship should make clear what practices will be visible in the lives of those who become disciples in your community of practice. The church council will need to discern what specific practices are characteristic of a disciple in their place and time. (Prayer? Worship? Stewardship? Service? Giving?)

Such a definition of discipleship is often called a "rule of life." One really simple one, often attributed to John Wesley, is "Do no harm. Do all the good you can. Attend to all the ordinances of God." Wesley's definition of discipleship was actually far more specific and robust, however, and included specific practices to be avoided or cultivated under each of those categories. These practices were highly contextual for the culture in which Wesley was embedded.

In our current missional context in America, to be a disciple is a counter-cultural way of living, but disciples are not to be so completely counter-cultural that they are isolated from their neighbors. Neither are they to be indistinguishable from their neighbors.

> *"I am not asking you to take them out of the world, but I ask you to protect them from the evil one. They do not belong to the world, just as I do not belong to the world. Sanctify them in the truth; your word is truth. As you have sent me into the world, so I have sent them into the world." (John 17:15-18)*

Your definition of the practices of a disciple should make clear both the ways in which we are distinguished from others (do not belong to the world) and the ways in which we are connected to others (sent into the world).

- **How will we do ministry in a manner that nurtures discipleship in our neighbors?** The church council will decide, in consultation with the pastor, what major strategies the congregation will employ in order both to grow as disciples and to reach the neighbors to whom God is sending them. In our changing contexts, this requires constant attention to whether or not what we are doing is fruitful. In a constantly changing mission context, our ministries cannot be assumed to be relevant and fruitful today no matter how well they worked before.

- **What are the boundaries that will focus our ministry in fulfillment of the mission and vision God has for our congregation?** The church council will determine the financial boundaries. The Council will establish policies for use of facilities, for safe sanctuary practices, and for employment. It should provide policy establishing the minimum qualifications for volunteer church leadership. It may set policies around how participants in the church are expected to behave toward one another (what are our values?). The council will delegate the implementation of these policies to the staff that manage the daily ministries of the congregation.

Why is governance important?

Every community of people is formed in the beginning around a mission. When my wife and I and our toddler arrived in Berkeley, California so I could start seminary, we needed people. In fact, we needed them immediately (to help us move our stuff - limited as it was - up to our third-floor walk-up apartment)!

> *When a congregation has lost its mission and vision, the only thing that can reinvigorate it is to find a renewed mission and vision. This rarely happens naturally or by accident.*

We also needed people to have Thanksgiving dinner with. We needed people to watch our first child, Justin, while Joanne was delivering our second child, Michael. We very quickly formed a deep community with two other families much like ours who also needed these things. Providing them for one another was the shared mission around which our community formed.

Sometimes, even today, it astounds me how far apart those three families have drifted as we have gone on to other stages of our lives. We three families who were so incredibly important to one another there in Berkeley now live scattered across the world. I hear of them through distant rumors. Our shared mission completed, and while we still regard one another as friends, we no longer share a deep community.

Any kind of community goes through that process of formation around a shared mission, maturation of the relationships and eventual decline in common purpose. Congregations are no exception. As the needs and commitments of people change, they diverge. Eventually all we hold common is that we like one another and share a history. That is not a compelling purpose for people who do not know us and who were not part of that history. We may stay together, but others will not join us.

When a congregation has lost its mission and vision, the only thing that can reinvigorate it is to find a renewed mission and vision. This rarely happens naturally or by accident. Someone must intentionally listen to God and to the congregation to discern if there is a compelling mission hidden in its midst that can renew its life together. If your congregation could discern it without leadership, they would already be busy accomplishing it!

Governance, as we are defining it here, is the responsibility of a specific leadership group at the core of congregational life to discern and articulate the mission and vision of the body by which God is calling it into the future. This group must also have the authority to focus the resources of the congregation in the direction of this calling. There is nothing more important to the vitality of a congregation than this.

A Simple Governance Structure

It is easy to cut your structure down to one committee. Many congregations have gotten there simply through an inability to get enough people to serve on all their committees. But this is not just about how many committees you have, it is much more about what your key leaders are responsible to accomplish. Here is a single-council structure designed to help you do governance in a manner that can liberate the missional energy of your congregation.

What are the characteristics of a leadership group capable of doing this work?

The Church Council
- **Will be constituted of no less than six and no more than fifteen members.** Councils with fewer than six persons will be unable to sustain the kinds of conversations necessary to do good governance. More than fifteen people will mean that some participants

aren't able to participate and that council conversations will lack focus and lead to more confusion than clarity.

- **Will be made up of leaders who have gifts and skills in listening and discernment, who are highly committed to the mission of the congregation, and who demonstrate the practices of discipleship in their daily lives.** Service on the council is not an honor; it is a responsibility. The council is responsible to the mission of the church and the members of the council should be people who are demonstrating commitment to the mission in their daily lives.

- **Will include members who are representative of the congregation.** Gifts, skills, commitment and discipleship should always trump demographic characteristics when building your council, but if you can't get anyone except old white men (or old white women, or young athletic men, or "insert homogeneous demographic here") to serve on your council your congregation is in trouble. It is especially important to include people who are relatively new to the congregation, but who are demonstrating significant commitment and interest.

- **Will meet infrequently.** Three to six meetings of the governing council per year produce the optimal environment for governance. When a council meets too often it almost inevitably gets distracted by management issues and fails to focus on the big picture. If your council members are concerned that infrequent meetings will not allow for timely decisions, you are probably focusing on management decisions, not governance. Your staff (paid and unpaid) will do the management (see Chapter Eight).

- **Will meet in a "retreat environment" and for at least four hours per meeting.** The conversations that lead to discernment of mission, vision, values and boundaries take longer than the customary hour-and-a-half or two-hour council meeting timeframe. They also require processes like appreciative inquiry and brainstorming that do not fit well in normal meeting processes. Getting out of the church building for these meetings actually helps the council to begin to think outside the limited concerns of the church community and to focus more intentionally on the mission.

Building Your Structure

If you are a United Methodist, you may want to refer to Appendix B where you will find a simple governance model that meets Disciplinary standards.

The ideal church council will look something like this: (11 members)

1. Council Chair (Lay Leader, President)

2. Pastor (just the lead/senior pastor if there is more than one)

3. Three people with skills and interest in finance and/or facilities

4. Three people with skills and interest in employment policy, teamwork, interpersonal relationships

5. Three people to fill out balance in the age, gender, and cultural diversity of the congregation.

Apart from the pastor, all the other members will be elected to three-year terms with about 1/3 of the members graduating in any given year. Four-year terms with 1/4 graduating each year can also work well.

> It is not "pastoral" to put or to keep someone on the council who is incapable of contributing to its work.

Typically, you would want council members to serve no more than two consecutive terms before taking a break from governance responsibility (and making room for new perspectives).

Avoid electing or designating "honorary" or "ex-oficio" members. Everyone on the council should be there to work at fulfilling its responsibility and purpose. *(Ex-officio indicates someone is representing some sub-group, but this work requires a perspective focused on the congregation as a whole.)*

You should adopt and enforce a "vacancy" policy that replaces someone on the council automatically at some minimum threshold of participation (such as missing half or more of the meetings in the previous twelve-month period). This is not a punitive policy, so it should not matter what the reason for chronic absence is – the functioning of the council requires that the members be present.

If a member has chronic health issues, for example, that prevent him from participating it does not make him a bad disciple, but it does prevent him from participating in fulfilling the responsibilities of a council member. It is not "pastoral" to put or to keep someone on the council who is incapable of contributing to its work.

Calling Members for Your Council

1. Use a "call process" to nominate leaders to the council. (A full description of a call process can be found in Chapter Six.)

2. The Council Chair is the most significant and demanding leadership position in the church. The chair should be a person with commitment to the church, adequate skills in group-process, and respect from the congregation for his or her discipleship.

3. The Council Chair and the Lead Pastor form a crucial partnership and should enjoy mutual regard and trust. If they do not, you should consider replacing the Chair, the Pastor or both.

4. All the members of the council should be called because of their discernment, Christian commitment, and passion for the mission of the church. They should be the best people you have available for this work and they should feel a personal calling to share in it.

5. If you cannot obtain enough of the right people for the council, leave spots blank rather than filling them with "placeholders" or last-choice participants. (You may also want to consider making the council smaller if it is not already at the lower limit of functioning.)

Meeting Schedule and Annual Agenda (5 meeting model)

In Appendix C you will find detailed agendas for a five-meeting annual cycle for a governing council. These are the basic purposes of a five-meetings in the schedule.

Each of these meetings except the All-Church Meeting will have about a five-hour time frame. Ideally, the council will meet somewhere other than the church in a setting that fosters earnest and open conversation. The council will share a meal as part of the process.

1. **Looking Up:** The first meeting of the year will orient your new council members to the mission, vision, values and boundaries of the congregation. This meeting is *formative*. It will also reorient your continuing members to these significant shared intentions. The council will review the mission, vision and values each year with an eye to whether or not they still articulate the shared intent of the congregation and the will of God.

   This session will also review the purpose of the council and the year-long cycle of work through which it fulfills its purpose. It should help new members of the council understand their responsibility on the council and how do they will do their work.

2. **Looking Back:** The second meeting of the year will look back over the previous year in the life of the congregation. This meeting is *evaluative*. What goals did we establish for that year? How did we do in fulfilling those goals? If we did fulfill them, are we happy with that? What will we do with our success? If we did not fulfill them, why not?

Did we fail to try? Did we try, but what we did just didn't work the way we thought? Were they ill-conceived goals in the first place? What can we learn from our failure? (How can we fail-forward?)

3. **Looking Around:** The third meeting of the year will take a snap shot of the congregation and community in their current reality. What is the situation of the church and community right now (about half way through the year)? This session will seek in every way to be *descriptive*. What is the state of our facilities, staff, finances, ministries, programs and discipleship in the congregation?

What is happening in our community that impacts our people and our mission field? How are the economy, the environment, and the culture in our mission field? We are not solving problems - we are simply seeking to listen to and see clearly our congregation and our community. This meeting is a time to assess the challenges and opportunities in our mission field and the strengths and weaknesses in our congregation.

4. **Looking Forward:** At this session the council will establish goals for the year ahead. This meeting is *motivating* and *focusing*. What one, two or three major things do we feel God is calling us to accomplish in the coming year? What ministries or programs need to be strengthened, expanded or started to accomplish those things? What ministries or programs have "run their course" and might be discontinued? How will we reallocate staff time and effort to address the focus we have identified? What will our budget be in light of our capacity and our focus in ministry?

155

5. **All-Church Meeting:** While it is not, strictly speaking, a meeting of the council, there should be an annual all-church meeting at which the council leads the congregation in considering and affirming its mission, vision, values and boundaries. The council will share an evaluation of the past year focused around the congregational goals. It will share the current state of the church. It will share the focal goals for the year ahead. It will present the budget (which may or may not be voted on). The entire congregation will also elect the leadership (council) it entrusts with the responsibility to lead it in fulfilling the goals established for the future.

The purpose of these meetings is to help the council lead the church through an annual governance cycle that is designed to continuously refine and recommit to the mission and vision.

GOVERNANCE CYCLE

Governing councils will need to pay attention to the life and spirit of the congregation all year long. This is why it is so essential that the council members actually be active and present in the life of the congregation. The council will also need to be intentional about listening to the congregation. Among the means that excellent church councils use to stay in touch with the congregation are:

- *Town Hall Meetings*: When there is a significant issue or decision the council may hold a town hall meeting (or meetings). These will be "single issue" meetings where the council can present their best thinking on the issue and then receive feedback (affirmations, concerns, and questions) from the congregation. These are not debates. No votes are taken. The council informs the congregation, listens to their input, and then leads the congregation based in that listening. This is holy conferencing.

- *Focus Groups*: Individual or small teams of council members visit various existing groups in the congregation (Sunday school classes, fellowship groups, ministry teams, etc.) or specifically invited small representative groups of people. As is the case with town hall meetings, the council members both share information and receive feedback on a particular issue.

- *Informal Conversations*: Council members will constantly engage in intentional conversations with individuals and groups at regular gatherings such as coffee hour following worship, and in the church groups they are involved in. In these conversations council members raise specific issues so that feedback can be received.

They will also be constantly attentive to what issues and concerns are arising in the congregation that may need council attention.

An example

At their third meeting of the year (looking around) the council learned that the children's ministry during the single Sunday morning worship was overcrowded and had no space to expand into. At the fourth meeting (looking forward) the council began to consider addressing this situation. They discussed whether to build a new addition to house more children's ministry space or to go to two worship services each Sunday in order to make more efficient use of the current space. The council members quickly realized that they weren't sure how the congregation would react to either of these alternatives.

They scheduled two town hall meetings at which they shared:
- The problem of overcrowding of children's ministry on Sunday mornings.
- The approximate process and costs of constructing additional space for children's ministries.
- The possible opportunities and threats they anticipated would be associated with going to two Sunday worship experiences.

They then invited each person at the town hall meetings to express their personal concerns, questions and affirmations about the possible solutions. Some of those attending also made some suggestions the council had not considered (purchase of the house next to the church for overflow space).

The council then held a special council meeting to consider the input from the congregation and to devise a specific plan to take to the congregation for approval.

Emergencies and Emerging Issues

Occasionally things will come up in the church that simply cannot be handled by the staff (management) without consultation with the council. Imagine the furnace dies. Replacing it is impossible within the normal maintenance budget. The pastor and facilities manager are not authorized to commit the funds necessary to address the problem.

When this kind of issue arises the pastor and or council chair may call a special emergency meeting of the council. The meeting will proceed with all the members of the council who are able to be present (sometimes the meeting can be held by email or conference call). The council will decide together what to do about the problem the congregation faces and may even call an all-church meeting if the matter is big enough to warrant that level of attention. Management issues, however, should hardly ever require an all-church meeting!

The Church Council and Policy

One of the important responsibilities of the church council is to set policy for the congregation. Policy is the primary way in which the council delegates management authority to the staff by establishing the boundaries within which the staff is free to operate without other approvals. In this sense, *policy should be understood primarily as a means of empowering staff to manage the ministries of the church* consistent with the values and mission of the congregation.

Policy should belong to the Church Council. That means that the Church Council can make changes in policy without requiring all-church votes or other approvals. The policy should specify what kind of council action is required to make a change in policy (for example, consideration at two meetings or a 2/3 vote of the council).

All of a church's policy should be gathered into a policy manual. Every key staff person and every council member should be provided with a copy of the policy manual. In addition, a policy manual will be available to anyone in the congregation who wants one. (It need not, however, be automatically distributed to everyone. Most people in the congregation will not care what the policies are; they will care whether things are working.) It is OK if your policy manual requires only two sides of a sheet of paper (though this will hardly ever be the case).

> *No matter what kind of church you are serving, the local church requires policy to provide clarity and focus for leaders and staff in implementing the mission of the local church. The idea is to create a church policy that prescribes how you actually do things in your congregation.*

It is best practice to adopt or amend policy only once each year (preferably at the "Looking Up" council meeting where mission, vision and practice are dealt with). Following this meeting a revised, updated version of the policy manual will be distributed.

160

If you fiddle with policy all the time, no one will know what the policy is. Policy that is too complicated or too extensive for your staff to remember and understand is worse than no policy at all.

For United Methodist Churches the beginning point for policy is The Discipline of the United Methodist Church. For other denominations there are varying degrees of denominational expectations, conditions and restrictions on local church policy. No matter what kind of church you are serving, the local church requires policy to provide clarity and focus for leaders and staff in implementing the mission of the local church. The idea is to create a church policy that, as a management document, prescribes how you actually do things in your congregation.

Here are some of the kinds of things that church councils should consider putting in policy. If your by-laws already specify some of these things, you still need to include them in the policy so that all the information is in one place.

- *What is the official structure* of our congregation? What elected boards, committees and offices do we have? What are the terms, forms of election, responsibilities and qualifications associated with these offices? Which decisions are reserved to elected bodies such as the church council or to an all-church meeting? Which decisions are reserved to the pastor or other key staff members?

- *What are the financial policies* we use to assure responsible and transparent management of the financial resources of the congregation? What are the restrictions on specific funds such as endowments or memorial funds, and who makes decisions about disbursement from them? (Every designated fund should have a distinct policy that makes clear what money is available from the fund, what uses are specified for the funds, and who can authorize spending from the fund.)

- *What are the safety and moral boundaries* that we consider essential to protect those who belong to, and those who are served by, our church? (Safe Sanctuary policies are required by almost all insurers of churches these days.)

- *What are the minimum expectations of members* of your church? What are the minimum expectations of those who serve as leaders of your church?

- *How are decisions made about use of church facilities?* Under what conditions can outside groups use the church and what kinds of restrictions will be placed on their use? Who decides about specific requests within the policy boundaries? What restrictions, if any, are placed on others using equipment or fixtures belonging to the church? What fees will be associated with use of facilities or equipment?

- *How do we designated the ministries of the church* as distinct from ministries that belong to individuals who happen to go to our church? How does something become "our ministry" or "our program"? (It is not a good idea to assume that if someone is a member of your church then everything good they do is automatically a ministry of the church.)

- *What are our employment policies* for paid staff? How do we handle vacation, leave and illness absences? What benefits are extended such as pension or health insurance? What is our expectation regarding paid staff and membership in the congregation? Who has authority for hiring and firing? What is the appeal or grievance process?

If your denomination provides policies or guidelines, you should start there. If what you find there does not address or exceeds your needs, seek policy examples from congregations similar in size to yours. State laws vary on financial, property and employment issues, so be sure to align your policies with local law.

It is always a bad idea to have a policy that your congregation cannot or will not adhere to. Be sure to consider whether your congregation can actually comply with a policy before you adopt it. If your policy manual is so long or so complicated that your staff and elected leaders can't understand it, start over and simplify. (This is one reason that even United Methodist congregations, who have The Discipline, need a policy. The Discipline is too much policy for any particular congregation.)

A good rule of thumb is not to have a particular policy unless your mission or your people is at significant risk by not being clear about this particular issue. You can always add a policy if you see a problem developing, but it is much harder to eliminate policies that have become neglected because they are irrelevant. Neglected policies are deadly to transparency and clarity and can increase legal liabilities.

Remember also that whatever is not prohibited or required by policy should be a matter of individual discretion. ***Be careful what you require but be clear about what you require.*** We live in a culture in which everyone has many choices. A congregation cannot survive without some shared convictions and practices to unite it. At the same time, our congregations cannot survive if their requirements have no apparent relevance to the people they are called to reach. As John Wesley famously said, "In essentials let us agree, in all else let it be think and let think."

Who writes policy?

Committees cannot write coherent policy. This is not a theory; it is a natural law - like gravity. People who are familiar with the problem that is calling for a policy should write the policy and recommend it to the council. The best policies have been "proven in practice" before they are "adopted as policy." Policy authors may be members of the council but need not be. The council will adopt and compile policy, but they can delegate the writing of policy to anyone who has the skill and knowledge to write it. Other congregations are potential sources of models for specific policies, but always look at two or three examples and then write one that meets your actual need.

The council bears the responsibility of ensuring that policies are not contradictory, irrelevant, confusing, or unenforceable. Always ask someone who might have to abide by a policy to read it and let you know what they think it requires of them before adopting it. It is actually best, whenever possible, to have people voluntarily abide by a policy long enough to see if it actually works before making it "official." No policy should become fully effective until the council adopts it and includes it in a policy handbook. Unwritten policy is deadly to transparency and clarity.

Church Council Problems

Implementing simple governance is always a somewhat confusing process. It is important to realize that our good mainline Protestant folks are not familiar with simple governance. They are used to a bureaucratic committee structure in which everyone expects to micro-manage everything. They are even less familiar with paying attention to clarity of mission, to fruitfulness, and adapting to a constantly changing mission environment. Don't be surprised if there are a few speed bumps on the road to effective governance.

> *It is important to realize that our good mainline Protestant folks are not familiar with simple governance. They are used to a bureaucratic committee structure in which everyone expects to micro-manage everything.*

We do not have enough qualified and willing persons to fill the council.

This will often appear to be the case when you first implement a simple governance model. **Above all, establish**

and retain high expectations for service on the council. The congregation will never demonstrate more commitment to Christ and his mission than those who lead it.

However, *you will do fine if you start with the best people you have.* These will be people who are committed to following God's calling in their own lives to the best of their ability and who want to see the church thrive. The chair will need to be among the most committed lay disciples in the congregation as well as someone who is really interested in uncovering the church's purpose (as opposed to imposing his/ her own) and humble enough to be willing to try something different in order to fulfill it.

If your structure calls for more people like that than you can find, then leave some positions vacant. Work on discipleship in the congregation. *If leaving a couple of positions vacant won't allow you to get a governing council established, you are not ready to address governance.* In that case, instead of implementing a new structure you should be focusing on discipleship with the people in your church. (And you should not expect to be inflicting your church on anyone else!)

We keep getting distracted by management issues

The most common problem for new governing councils is that they are easily distracted from attention to governance by issues of management. A typical example would be that someone mentions at the "looking around" meeting that the roof is approaching the limit of its useful life. As soon as that descriptive reality is offered, someone will say something like,

"Well I hope we use metal roofing next time!" The next person to speak says, "Only if they can get a color that doesn't clash with the brick." Before you know it, the council has spent a half-hour discussing every detail of the roofing issue. They have diverted to management and governance is lost.

"Reporting" is another way that management issues can distract the council from their responsibility to govern. Persons on the council want to share what their ministries are doing and feel that they need to hear what others are doing. This is management (alignment and coordination) and is not the domain of the council. Communication of the ministries of the congregation needs to be shared with everyone, not just the council. It is a staff function to manage the information flow so that the right people get the right information at the right time.

To avoid falling into these traps the council should have a very clear agenda with specific questions to discuss. The chair should be very familiar with the agenda, why it is important, and diligent in keeping the council on task.

It is often helpful to have a person sit with the council whose sole responsibility is calling it to their attention when they get off track. The "process person" monitors what the council are doing and discussing. Whenever they begin to depart from the agenda (especially by shifting to management) the monitor stops the meeting briefly. One way to do this is to simply ring a pleasant-sounding bell and everyone stops for 30 seconds to ask themselves silently, "what are we doing right now and is it our responsibility?" Then the meeting resumes.

Disconnection of the council from the congregation

When governance is working well the council becomes a very rewarding and engaging community for the people involved. They are having deep conversations about God's purpose for their church, about the value and promise of their church, and about the character of their community and the needs of their neighbors. You will soon find that people look forward to these meetings!

Too many congregations resolve difficult disagreements about issues in the church by giving up on fruitfulness and purpose just to keep the peace. Too many others resolve them by getting rid of the pastor.

There is a risk that the high level of relationship and trust that council members develop with one another will erode their commitment to really engage with the rest of the people of the church and community. There can be a temptation for the council to begin to think, "we know best."

There are several practices that can help offset this natural tendency. The "looking around" session of the council each year should focus on information that council members have individually gathered as each of them has listened to specific parts of the church and community. One council member may, for example, have interviewed the small group leaders to see what challenges and rewards they are experiencing in their ministries. That council member may also have collected three stories from the local paper that represent emerging issues in the community. Other council members will have also prepared by listening to the church and community in other ways.

Another important protection against the isolation of the council is the annual all-church meeting. This meeting requires that the council interpret its work to the congregation as a whole. It is a format for a conversation between the council and the church around purpose, strategy, and outcomes. This should be a very significant moment in the life of the congregation every year; indeed, it should be a high point.

Finally, if your council has not found any reason to hold a town hall meeting or a focus group process around a specific issue in the past year, then you need to ask yourselves why not. Every year the council should be dealing with issues significant enough to warrant an intentional listening process with the congregation. Has your council stopped asking big questions? Does your council trust itself too much and the congregation not enough?

We have conflict between the council or council chair and pastor.

Too many congregations resolve difficult disagreements about issues in the church by giving up on fruitfulness and purpose just to keep the peace. Too many others resolve them by getting rid of the pastor.
Your pastor and your council must share a common vision for your church. This common vision will be discerned through

serious and sometimes difficult conversations. Honesty, mutual trust, and a commitment to work through heartfelt disagreements will be essential. This work requires that both the pastor and the council believe that the mission is more important than their personal comfort. However, if anyone involved is stuck in a conflict they are unwilling to resolve, the church will also be stuck until there is a change in the leadership team. Fruitful councils are made up of people, both lay and clergy, who trust a faithful process more than they trust their personal opinions. (See, *The Anatomy of Peace*, Arbinger Institute, for excellent conflict resolution practices.)

Congregations that lack a focus on a God-given purpose accumulate people who are there for purposes of their own. Ultimately, this perpetuates a lack of focus and fruitfulness. This is the reality in most stable and declining congregations. Everyone has their own reason for being there, but they have no compelling shared reason.

> *...if you do not have a focused, compelling and godly mission and vision, no fiddling with structure or change of pastor will make any difference.*

Renewed fruitfulness will only come with a renewed focus, and this will always create a certain amount of conflict among people who have different ideas about what goals should take precedence. When this is the case, getting rid of the pastor will often be on the table and will seldom help solve the problem.

If your congregation is struggling to identify a unifying and motivating mission, you will need to look for a different book than this one to help you enter a season of mission and vision discernment. Many people are skeptical of vision processes, having gone through the whole "flip-chart and sticky-note retreat" too many times with too little consequence. I understand. But if you do not have a focused, compelling and godly mission and vision, no fiddling with structure or change of pastor will make any difference. A congregation without a unifying and inspiring common mission is a dying congregation (though dying often takes a very long time).

If your congregation and your council continue to struggle to come to a compelling common mission and vision you are really faced with two alternatives:

- You can engage a capable and experienced consultant or intentional interim pastor to help your council through the process of discerning and articulating a compelling mission and vision. And then you must risk losing a few (sometimes key) people in the congregation who do not consent to the new clarity.
- You can continue without a clear mission and vision and this will lead ultimately to the decline and death of the congregation.

Implementing a simple governance structure in your church will be hard work. If your church is not ready to do that work, it doesn't mean there is nothing you can do.

You can begin to pay attention to good leadership practices (aligning responsibility, authority and accountability) in your existing organizational structure and it will help.

You can help the existing central body in your system begin to pay attention to issues of mission, vision and values without adopting a new structure.

You can drop back to the real basic work of leading your people from "church membership" to discipleship.

All these will help. Most church leaders find that, if they do those kinds of things eventually their tall, complicated structure begins to get in the way. That is when implementing a simple governance structure is most useful.

You can start where you are.

Study Questions

1. What person or body in your church is responsible for discerning and articulating your unifying mission, vision and values?

2. What are the unifying mission, vision and values of your congregation?

3. Do your ministries and programs align with and fulfill that vision and do they function according to those values?

4. What do you find most promising about a Council doing the kind of work described in this chapter?

5. What do you find most threatening or impractical about having a Council do this kind of work in your congregation?

Chapter Eight
The Staff

When we talk about the categories of work in our churches we typically make a distinction between staff (the people who get paid for their church work) and volunteers, the people who do not get paid for their church work. This is not a helpful distinction, because it focuses our attention on whether someone is paid or not, and whether they are doing church work or not. What we need to be focused on is whether or not people are in ministry rather than whether or not they are doing church work. And we need to pay attention to the order of ministry they are doing (governance, management, or direct ministry) instead of whether they are being paid or not.

Vital churches do not make a significant distinction between paid and unpaid people. What they understand is that the important distinction is the one between those who are responsible for leading ministries and those who are doing direct ministry. In simple governance we refer to those who are leading ministries as "staff," whether they are paid or unpaid. And we refer to those who are doing direct ministry as disciples, whether they are paid or unpaid.

In this chapter we will look at the responsibility of the staff. We will also look at some of the best practices and the kind of organizations that make the most of staff.

Remember the Principles for Effective Leadership!

Throughout our consideration of staff, it is important to focus intently on the principles that guide us in a fruitful use of leadership. Just take a moment right now to recall that we will need to align and balance *responsibility, authority, and accountability* as we create staff positions and as we call leaders to serve in them.

> *We refer to those who are leading ministries as "staff," whether they are paid or unpaid. And we refer to those who are doing direct ministry as "disciples," whether they are paid or unpaid.*

Your staff members (paid and unpaid!) are essential to a fruitful expression of the mission, vision and values of the congregation through the ministries it carries out. No matter how excellent and faithful the "doers" may be; your congregation will not be fruitful in ministry unless you have some capable leaders and you put them into service in ways that allow their leadership to be effective. Use a call system like that described in Chapter Six to select and assign people in leadership.

Each staff person deserves to have a responsibility that is clear about the required outcomes and about the way it fits the core mission, vision and values of the congregation as a whole. Every staff person deserves to be delegated the authority necessary to be able to fulfill that responsibility. Finally, every staff member deserves to know to whom and by what process he or she will be accountable for the responsibility assigned.

176

The Special Responsibility of the Pastor

Every church has ministry teams and ministry team leaders. We know this because stuff (worship, potlucks, classes, rummage sales, mission trips, newsletters, websites) is happening. Not every church is effective in mission, however. We know this because some churches are dying. One important difference between the churches that thrive and the churches that die is this; the churches that thrive have a pastoral leader who fulfills the responsibility of aligning the ministry teams with the mission, vision and values of the congregation as a whole.

It is the responsibility of the governing council to discern and articulate the mission, vision and values of the congregation. It is the responsibility of the staff to manage the ministry teams that embody the mission vision and values. It is the responsibility of the pastor to align the staff (and through them the ministry teams) in their work. Alignment is really the outcome of effective accountability. We ask of every staff person and every ministry, "Are we accomplishing what we have been called to do?"

The pastor carries out this alignment through working with the ministry team leaders. The pastor is the chief of staff.

A brief aside: in churches smaller than about 50 in average worship attendance, someone will serve as the person who articulates the mission and aligns everyone to that mission, but often it is not the pastor. Pastors tend to come and go in these churches and often serve less than full time. Since maintaining effective alignment depends on a deep

> *One important difference between the churches that thrive and the churches that die is this; the churches that thrive have a pastoral leader who fulfills the responsibility of aligning the ministry teams with the mission, vision and values of the congregation as a whole.*

understanding of the particular gifts of the congregation and the context of ministry, pastors have less influence than long-time members. In these smallest congregations the person bringing alignment will often be the most strong-willed, and hopefully the most spiritually mature, person in the church.

Still, in most congregations the pastor must be the person who bears responsibility for the alignment of ministries. This is because the role of the pastor is the only role in the church that has the essential characteristics necessary to fulfill this responsibility:

- The pastor is the most effective bridge between the governing council and the staff. It is via this bridge that the mission and vision are constantly conveyed to the ministries of the congregation. If there are several bridges between the council and staff, then nobody will know to whom they are accountable. (Staff cannot be accountable to the council. The council is simply unable to provide the consistent engagement necessary for useful accountability.)
- The pastor is usually the person who sees and participates in the broadest aspect of the life of the congregation on a regular basis. Seldom does anyone but the pastor has the access and influence with the congregation required to sustain alignment of its ministries. If the pastor is not leading the congregation

in alignment, alignment will almost certainly decrease, and individual programs will become the focus of loyalty for special interest groups in the congregation.

How do pastors align ministry?

Pastors who align the ministries of their congregation use a variety of methods in accomplishing this responsibility. Alignment of a congregation to its mission and purpose permeates every aspect of the pastor's engagement with the congregation and community: preaching, casual conversation, pastoral, teaching, community involvement – every aspect of the pastor's ministry.

Pastors cannot succeed in this responsibility, no matter how dedicated and talented, if the congregation will not allow them the authority necessary. The essential authority required for pastors to succeed is that afforded a chief of staff. Each person leading a ministry team of the congregation should be very clear that they are accountable to the pastor for the responsibility with which they have been entrusted.

> *The alignment of a congregation to mission, vision and values is not an event on the church's calendar; it is a matter of twenty-four-seven attention.*

The pastor will be accountable to the governing council to lead the church in fulfilling its mission, vision and values as they are expressed in the goals set forth by the council. All other ministry leaders (staff) will be accountable to the pastor for their part in fulfilling these goals.

179

Giving the pastor the essential authority is, of course, not enough to guarantee fruitfulness. While leadership is essential, it is also essential that it be good leadership.

Effective pastoral leaders keep the goals in first place.

Effective pastoral leaders build a sense of common purpose in their staff (paid and unpaid) by constantly keeping the mission, vision and values of the congregation as the standard by which everything is measured.

Eventually, some leaders will reveal themselves to be truly in opposition to the mission, vision and values that really belong to your congregation. When that happens deal with these people as "misplaced" in your congregation and help them find somewhere else that better fits their aspirations.

The pastor applies this standard most consistently to her or himself and is intentionally transparent in that commitment. It does wonders for a staff and congregation when a pastor is open about both his or her successes and failures in contributing to the fulfillment of the mission and vision of the congregation. It becomes clear to all that the pastor is accountable to the mission and so are they.

The pastor also constantly makes the connection between the responsibility of each staff member and the overall goals of the congregation. Never assume that ministry team leaders already know this! Always ask of everything your staff is doing, "Is this helping us to fulfill the mission we share?" Then frequently affirm the ways in which you see staff and ministry teams contributing to the overall mission of the congregation. Do this publicly and often.

Effective pastoral leaders start with the people they have and nurture them toward excellence together.

If you are the pastor of a church that is not thriving, do not assume it is because your people are not high commitment disciples. It is more likely that they are just struggling to do their ministries in the absence of effective alignment. Work with your people to discover their common aspirations. Help them to discover what role each of them is passionate and gifted to fulfill. Encourage them to withdraw from responsibilities that do not fit their gifts and to focus on challenges that do.

Do not try to accomplish anything (no matter how essential you think it may be) if there isn't someone feeling a personal calling to that responsibility. Let some things go that have been done in the past if they are not supported anymore. Remember that real support is participation, not expression that "someone should be doing this." Eventually a congregation will align to its core ministries if the pastor will help the congregation let go of intensive care for dying ministries.

Defend your ministry leaders from the expectations of others when those expectations do not honor their gifts or are irrelevant to the mission. Congregations are often driven more by past successes (usually nostalgically enhanced) than they are by current mission. They will want their leaders to "keep things going." They will complain that someone isn't doing it the way they remember. You must defend your staff from this constant and depressing feedback. And you must constantly lift up for everyone the stories of successful fulfillment of the mission and purpose.

Eventually, some leaders may reveal themselves to be truly in opposition to the mission, vision and values that actually belong to your congregation. When that happens deal with these people as "misplaced" in your congregation and help them find somewhere that better fits their aspirations (even if that is another congregation). Absolutely do NOT follow that horribly misguided notion that getting someone involved in leadership will bring him or her around! Putting a dissenter in leadership will only destroy alignment, corrupt the mission and dishearten your people.

Effective pastors nurture excellent communication with their staff.

> *As the chief of staff, an effective pastor understands that staying in real connection with the staff, including an up to date knowledge of how they are experiencing their ministry area, is the most important work of all.*

Effective pastors sustain excellent communication and understanding with and between the members of their staff. Ironically, many pastors communicate extensively with their congregation (Sermons, teaching, newsletter) while virtually ignoring their staff. We have a tendency to assume that our key staff people can "take care of themselves" and that they "know what's going on." Effective pastoral leaders reverse this priority.

Your responsibility to your staff includes inspiring them in the goals they have set, equipping them with the authority they need, and keeping in touch with how they are doing. Whenever you can, you want to be able to step in with encouragement and redirection when the issues are small, not wait until there is a blow-up or despair. Your staff will then become a significant means by which commitment to the mission and purpose is communicated to the congregation as a whole.

You will want to have a regular (weekly?) staff meeting with staff members who lead teams that impact the daily life of the whole church. Staff persons responsible for calendar, facilities, finance, and major weekly programs such as worship will certainly need to be together on a very regular basis to discuss and decide how their various efforts are going and how they can be coordinated in ways that make them more effective.

You will want to have less frequent, but equally regular, gatherings of a broader base of leaders who bear responsibility for the less comprehensive ministries. Some ministry team leaders may be best integrated into the core ministry of the congregation simply by an occasional phone conversation with the pastor about how their ministry is going and what it is accomplishing. You should have at least an annual gathering of all ministry team leaders to be affirmed for their leadership, to share their struggles and successes, and to rehearse the common mission that unites them.

The key is to ask, "How often do which leaders need to communicate to sustain a team of leaders capable of helping our congregation fulfill God's will for us together?" Whatever pattern of meetings or communications you establish, regularly evaluate whether these include the right people with the right frequency to sustain excellent staff integration with the purpose of the church. If participation in the meetings drops off, make adjustments. If alignment is being lost, increase the effort.

If this sounds like too many meetings, remember this – none of these ministry teams is a committee. Some of them may not be having meetings at all. Others may meet rarely to plan their work together. The alignment you arrange is essential to keeping them coordinated and connected.

Every group of people who does anything on behalf of the church is a ministry team. Every ministry team has a leader. And every ministry team leader is a staff person (whether paid or volunteer).

Even when you have an effective system of staff communication, you must remain aware that a major part of this alignment work will be done completely apart from any formal meetings. "Management by walking around" is gaining in credibility because it puts the chief of staff in the places where alignment can be carried out naturally and in small ways.

As the chief of staff, an effective pastor understands that staying in real connection with the staff, including an up to date knowledge of how they are experiencing their ministry responsibility, is very important work. This is what it means *"to equip the saints for the work of ministry, for building up the body of Christ, until all of us come to the unity of the faith and of the knowledge of the Son of God, to maturity, to the measure of the full stature of Christ." (Ephesians 4:12-13)*

The Responsibility of Staff

A person will be considered to be on staff if he or she has responsibility for leading a group of people in carrying out a ministry of the congregation. (Do not confuse individuals who do important work by themselves with staff members. Staff members are people who are responsible for leading at least two other people in doing a ministry.)

Every group of people that does anything on behalf of the church is a ministry team. Every ministry team has a leader. And every ministry team leader is a staff person.

In vital congregations, many ministries are initiated by the people who end up being the ministry team.

The responsibility shared by all staff persons is to call, equip and coordinate a team of disciples in fulfilling the ministry responsibility that has been entrusted to them.

It sounds clear. It is clear if the congregation has provided a clear statement of the ministry.

Defining a ministry

In vital congregations, many ministries are actually initiated by the people who end up being the ministry team. When this is the case the ministry team leader will need to create a clear ministry description. Even when a ministry team leader is being called to accept a preexisting leadership position, he or she should demand that the ministry be clearly described. Part of the alignment role of the pastor is maintaining a kind of list of the "ministries of the church." Each ministry on the list should have a description. A clear ministry description will include the following elements:

There is a clear statement of the ministry responsibility.
- Who is the mission field being addressed? Who do we want to reach?
- What is the impact we seek to have in the life of those we are seeking to reach?
- How will we know if we are succeeding in reaching that mission field with that outcome? What are the measures of effectiveness for this ministry?
- What is the method we intend to use to accomplish this ministry?

There is a clear statement of authority.
- What funds, facilities, and human resources are delegated or provided to the ministry team to work with?
- What boundaries (if any) limit the authority of the ministry team to raise funds on their own, use facilities, and call people to the ministry team?

- What other boundaries or expectations are in effect for this ministry team (safe sanctuary policy, date or time expectations, behavioral, etc.)?

There is a clear statement of accountability.
- How does this ministry contribute and connect to the overall mission, vision, values and goals of the congregation?
- Who is the person to whom this staff person is accountable? (This will be the pastor unless this ministry team functions as a part of some other ministry team or staff position. Multiple "layers" of accountability should be avoided but become necessary as the number of ministries grows.)
- What are the parameters for evaluation? (These come from the "How will we know we are successful?" answer in the responsibility description.)

There is actually a team.
- Really! List the people who are on the team.

Here is an example of a ministry description that meets these criteria. You have seen one before (for the facilities manager). This one is a more of a program ministry.

Sunday Morning Children's Ministry
Our Sunday morning children's ministry is for children between 3 and 10 years old and who are present during the worship services on Sunday morning.

Our goals for ministry with these children are:
- To provide a safe, welcoming environment parents will feel comfortable entrusting their children to while they participate in worship.
- To familiarize children, in a manner appropriate to their age-level, with the fact that they are children of God, beloved without condition.
- To help children to understand themselves as ministers of the love of God to others and to experience the joy of being a blessing.
- To engage children in an age appropriate manner with the scriptures (especially the primary stories and characters) being used in worship that week so that they may begin to see the Bible and the faith as relevant in their lives.

We evaluate the effectiveness of our children's ministry by:
- At least 90% of parents who attend worship with us entrust their children to this ministry.
- Evaluations by parents indicate that their children like to come and want to come back.
- Evaluations by parents indicate this ministry as one reason they have chosen our church.
- Parents report that their children can engage with them each week about the scripture used that day in worship.

Our core methodology for Sunday morning children's ministry is:
- Utilization of multi-sensory, activity-based learning (songs, games, art, play, service).
- Focused on each week's scripture and general worship theme in a manner appropriate for children.
- Strict adherence to our safe sanctuary policies.

Resource commitments / boundaries
- Sunday morning children's ministry has use of the fireside room and classrooms #3,4,5 and 6 from 8 AM to 1 PM every Sunday morning from September 1 to June 15.
- The budget for this ministry is $2000 for this program year.
- Every activity of this ministry must adhere strictly to our safe sanctuary policy. Children are a vulnerable and sacred trust and their wellbeing is our first priority.
- No children may be admitted to the program without being registered by a parent or legal guardian.
- Ministry Team members must each pass a background check (every three years) and be interviewed by the team leader for suitability for service with small children. They must also be regular participants in a primary spiritual growth aspect of our church (worship or small group).

- The Children's Sunday Morning Ministry team is led by John Smith and is accountable to the pastor.
- Evaluation of the ministry will be driven by the evaluation form completed by parents, and by the percentage of parents in worship who entrust their children to this ministry.

Once there is a clear ministry description, the staff person then has the responsibility of calling the disciples who will constitute the ministry team that will carry out this responsibility. There are two very different

> *Ministry team leaders must always remember that a core responsibility is to equip and coordinate the disciples on their ministry team so that they can all be fruitful in fulfilling their ministry.*

ways to proceed and either can be very effective.

Building a ministry team – method one.

1. The ministry team leader begins by outlining the ministry to be initiated. Let's use a simple example: The ministry team will serve lunch to the church council members at their four quarterly meetings. Most of the ministry description elements are pretty obvious for this ministry, so I will not go into that detail. You can see an example of a much more elaborate ministry description above.

2. The ministry team leader then uses a call system, where the whole ministry description is the job description to which all of them are called. The ministry team leader will obtain commitments from the people he would like to work with on this ministry.

3. The ministry team leader then gathers the team and, together, they plan the details of how they will fulfill the

ministry description. For example: What will the menus be? How much will the meals cost? What are the details (decorations, serving location, cooking, etc.)? Which team members will do which tasks for which meetings?

4. The discussion in section 3 results in the individual team member job descriptions (which may or may not be specifically written down depending on how complex the ministry is).

5. The ministry team leader will get the necessary approvals from the pastor (or another accountability person designated when he was called to this task). For example, do we have the budget requested? Can we use the room we plan to serve in? Once this approval is granted the ministry team leader is free to carry out the ministry without further approvals.

Building a ministry team – method two.

1. The ministry team leader either receives or creates a complete and thorough ministry description that has been approved for launch (such as the Sunday Children's Ministry example).

2. The ministry team leader develops a plan for a ministry team that breaks the entire ministry down into a number of team position descriptions. These are like job descriptions that include the responsibilities in each position including the amount of time commitment involved, the tasks, the duration of the commitment and so on.

3. With the entire team design in place, the ministry team leader alone (or better, with a small group of helpers) goes through a call process for each team position.
4. When the full team is called, the ministry team leader can launch the ministry. (Do not launch a ministry without the minimum team necessary for effective ministry!)

Sustaining the Ministry

Too many ministry team leaders get so caught up in the performance of the ministry that they neglect the maintenance of the ministry team. Ministry team leaders must always remember that a core responsibility is to equip and coordinate the disciples on their ministry team so that they can fulfill their ministry.

Ministry team leaders can help equip the disciples on their teams is a variety of ways.

Ministry team leaders nurture disciples when they ask:
* How is our ministry doing? Does it seem to be reaching the people we are seeking to be in ministry with? Is it showing signs of accomplishing the outcomes in their lives we are hoping for? (Be sure you are actually gathering real answers, not just discussing with your team what you all think!)
* What stories are we seeing and hearing that illustrate the fruitfulness of this ministry?
* How are my team members doing? Are any showing signs of withdrawing, exhaustion, or ineffectiveness? Are any showing signs that they desire more challenge or greater responsibility? Who is thriving and growing?

Who is misplaced in this ministry and how can I help them move to something more aligned with their gifts?

- How can the larger congregation beyond this ministry experience it, know about it, and support it?
- How can the community beyond the church know this ministry and what do they think of our effort?
- Are there people who are not being touched by this ministry that we could be reaching?

Ministry team leaders support their teams when:

- Ministry team members are repeatedly reminded of the significance of this ministry in the overall mission of the congregation. How do we fit in with everyone else in our church to fulfill the call of Christ?
- Team members have opportunities to provide feedback and suggestions for improving the ministry methods.
- The mission community (those we are trying to be in ministry with) have opportunities to provide feedback about how they experience the ministry and what impact it is having in their lives.
- Team members are receiving support and encouragement, and where appropriate, have relevant adjustments made in their responsibilities. Are your team members continuing to grow in truth and grace into the likeness of Jesus Christ?
- They attend to their personal spiritual health and growth, and step back if the demands of the responsibility become unsustainable for any reason.
- They provide honest and considered input to the pastor about the sustainability and fruitfulness of the ministry and of their leadership. If changes in the expectations of

this ministry are needed the ministry team leader should raise them so that adjustments can be made while the ministry is still viable.

- They are open and responsive when the accountability process reveals that adjustments may be necessary for the ministry to remain fruitful and/or to realign it to the overall goals of the congregation.

The bottom line is making disciples of Jesus Christ for the transformation of the world (or whatever your mission is).

It's amazing how easy it is for our ministry programs to completely overwhelm our ministry goals. We get so immersed in what we are doing that we can completely lose sight of why we were doing it in the first place. One of the most important responsibilities of the staff is to keep reminding the congregation that everything we do is for the purpose of furthering God's intentions for our church, our community, the world and us. Surely this is what it means to proclaim God as our sovereign and to seek to live in the realm of God.

In the church, the purposes of God for us certainly include helping people to become disciples (students) of Jesus Christ. So, a final word in this chapter on the responsibility of staff. Almost everything you have read here has focused on how to be effective in implementing and sustaining ministries. But all the while we are doing that, underneath it all, lays this timeless agenda of the Holy Spirit, which is to bring everyone to the likeness of Jesus. That means not just serving people but helping them to begin to discover their own identity as servants, and not just blessing people but helping them to discover their power to bless.

With that in view, perhaps the simplest and most basic responsibility of pastors and all our church leaders is to constantly find ways to give away their ministry responsibilities to others who have not yet discovered that they, too, are entitled to the privilege and joy of being ministers of Jesus Christ and his grace for the world. Who are you calling into the life of ministry?

Study Questions

1. What is most promising and compelling to you about this way of thinking about ministry team leadership?

2. Does your congregation make a significant distinction between paid staff and volunteer leaders? If yes, what do you find most interesting and most threatening about shifting to this view of the role of staff in your congregation?

3. Is your pastor functioning as chief of staff in your congregation? If not, who is responsible for aligning and coordinating your ministries to fulfill your mission, vision and values?

    a. What do you see as the value in having the pastor serve as chief of staff?

    b. What do you see as the threat to having the pastor serve as chief of staff?

4. Make a list of the "things that are happening in our church" and see if you can identify the ministry team leader for each of these events, activities or ministries.

   a. Are these leaders explicitly acknowledged as leaders by your congregation?

   b. Do these leaders have a fruitful balance of responsibility, authority and accountability?

Chapter Nine
Ministry Teams

Much of what needs to be said about how ministry teams are formed and how they function has been covered in Chapter Eight on the responsibility of staff. In this chapter we will focus especially on what the responsibility of a ministry team member looks like. Here, we begin looking at something like a practical definition of a disciple.

One of the most frequently repeated phrases coming from the lips of Jesus is, "follow me." It occurs twenty-one times in the NRSV version of the Gospels beginning with Matthew 4:19 and sprinkled throughout to John 21:22. We understand Jesus to be the incarnation (embodiment) of God.

> *The purpose of all we have said about leadership and organization comes down to this: it is to embody the life of Jesus in our lives as we help the people in and beyond our churches to embody the mission of Jesus Christ in their lives.*

It follows that Jesus intended his disciples to be the incarnation of his mission to the world. That is what he meant by the invitation to follow him. Discipleship will certainly impact what we think, but it is really most present in what we do.

The purpose of all we have said about leadership and organization comes down to this: it is to embody the life of Jesus in our lives as we help the people in and beyond our churches to embody the mission of Jesus Christ in their lives. It is to make disciples of Jesus Christ for the transformation of the world. It is to transform the world into the likeness of the realm of God through the transformation of people into the likeness of Jesus Christ.

Ministry teams are the places where people embody the ministry of Jesus in specific and concrete ways. Ministry teams are the literal expression of discipleship. Ideally, every person in a church will be in some ministry team. If you ask them, "What is your ministry?" they will immediately and confidently answer.

It is very important for us to remember that *not all ministries and not all ministry teams are focused on doing church work*. In vital churches most of the ministry teams and most of the people will be engaged in ministry that is expressed outside the church. Habitat for Humanity ministry teams, food bank ministry teams, public school support ministry teams, mental health service teams, emergency relief ministry teams, carbon footprint reduction ministry teams: these are all embodiments of the mission of Jesus (as are countless others).

We want to take care to help our people assure that ministries like these give glory to Christ. This works best when those doing ministry do it as a team, and when people receiving the benefit of the ministry know that it is Christ's people doing it because he has called us to do it.

A vital congregation has a culture in which everyone desires to be a disciple, expects to be a disciple, and experiences a continual growth in their understanding and expression of their own discipleship.

Characteristics of Disciples

It's not about me.

Disciples are people who have been captured by the realization that their real life is found as a participant in God's life. In Rick Warren's book, *The Purpose Driven Life*, the first chapter is entitled "It's All About God," and the first words are "It's not about you." There is much in Rick Warren's theology that I might disagree with, but I certainly share his conviction that this is the fundamental realization that motivates the life of a disciple.

If it isn't about me, then what is it about? Our culture and human history provide many possible and popular answers: family,

> *Discipleship will certainly impact what we think, but it is really most evident in what we do.*

work, nation, tribe, money, pleasure, happiness, even church. The list can go on and on. Disciples are people who find even the most valuable of those answers ultimately inadequate and unsatisfying. Disciples are people who agree that the only adequate answer to the question, "What is it all about?" comes from God in Jesus Christ. Disciples are people who invest their lives in the answer, "It's about the mission of God to the world as we see it in Jesus."

A disciple is a person who relates to the congregation and to the ministry team on which he or she serves from the perspective of God's mission in Jesus Christ. Disciples do not evaluate the church on the basis of whether or not they "like it," but on the basis of whether or not it is expressing the mission of Jesus in our time and place. Disciples are invested in the character of the mission of Jesus here and now, and their place in that mission. They are much less concerned about whether their particular tastes and preferences are being fulfilled than whether their ministry is effective for the mission of Jesus to the world.

Several years ago, I complimented a pastoral colleague on the fruitfulness of his leadership in doubling the size of his congregation in just about six years. He said something to me that struck me to the core. He said, "You don't understand what drives this congregation. It's not me. When I was hired here the leaders in the congregation, almost all of them retirement age, told me not to lead them to be the church they desire, but to become the one that could make disciples of their grandchildren." Those were disciples!

It is about my passion and gifts.

To say that it is not about you is not to say that you don't matter! Sure, it's a cliché, but no two people are alike. The cliché reveals something about the core character of the creator. Apparently, God loves diversity! So, as you develop as a disciple it will be important for you to grow more deeply self-aware of what you are good at and what you are not good at. You will become more and more rooted in what concerns you most, and what inspires you most.

As you seek to find the ministry and ministry team you are truly called into you should seek out those ministries that connect your passion and your gifts with the core purpose of your church and the specific needs of your neighbors. This is what it means to express the greatest commandment, "You shall love the Lord your God with all your heart, soul, mind and strength, and your neighbor as yourself." Disciples never say, "If no one else will do it, then I guess I could." Instead they will take on any responsibility in the congregation only with this conviction, "Yes, I feel that this is a responsibility that God is calling me to fulfill at this time, and I will undertake it as a holy calling."

Discipleship is a process not a status.

It is a serious mistake when we let a responsibility own us. God alone deserves our ultimate loyalty. So, we need to remember that following and serving Jesus is a lifelong process in which we never stop learning. This means that there is no shame in deciding that a responsibility in ministry that we took on at one point in our journey of discipleship may not be the one God intends for us at a later point in that journey.

It is a difficult, but profoundly holy, witness to say to our church, "I have been doing this for a while, but it is no longer what I am called to do." We may often realize a shift in our callings at times that do not match three-year election cycles. Neither do they always match the appearance of another leader who is stepping up to the particular responsibility we are abandoning. And, most difficult of all, these moments of abandoning may not be accompanied by any crystal clarity about what is coming next.

A radical trust in God's presence with us sometimes requires that we step off one step before we are really sure where the next step will be found. A wise guy once said, "You can't get to second base until you take your foot off first base." Disciples need to be able to step away from their current ministry without necessarily stepping directly into another.

Sometimes there will need to be a fallow season before the next calling is clear. But disciples never quit seeking a way to be engaged in the mission of Jesus, and they never quit engaging in the community of faith as a support and encouragement for that quest.

The ministry of a disciple may go through twists and turns, times of activity and times of reflection. But disciples always remain in the body of Christ. Too often our "work ethic" culture makes people feel so ashamed of their need for a break that they have to leave the church just to get one. That is a profoundly unnecessary and tragic occurrence. We need to teach people that sabbatical is part of the rhythm of faith. Our church leaders must not ask more of people than God asks of them.

You never retire from discipleship.

When someone realizes that their calling is no longer chairing the church council, or leading the children's ministry, it does not mean they are retiring from ministry. The question for all of us who still breathe is, "What is it that I can do to participate in the mission of my church with the gifts and abilities that I have now?"

One day I was visiting a shut-in woman in a small-town congregation I was serving. I had noticed a spiral notebook beside her chair on a couple of previous visits. I could see that the pages were covered with rows and columns and checkmarks.

> *Sometimes there will need to be a fallow season before the next calling is clear. But disciples never quit seeking a way to be engaged in the mission of Jesus, and they never quit engaging in the community of faith as a support and encouragement for that quest.*

Finally, I asked her, "What is that notebook you keep by your chair?"

She answered, "Those are my widows."

"What do you mean, your widows?"

"These are the widows in our town who live alone. I call each one every day to ask how they are doing and chat a little bit. If one of them doesn't answer after a couple of tries, and I haven't heard that they were going to be out or away, then I follow up with family or even the local police to make sure that they are OK. And, of course, I pray for each of them every day."

This woman never let any circumstance of her life, even being confined to her home by poor health, limit her sense of mission. Disciples never retire, even though their callings change.

> **Serving on Ministry Teams**
>
> The people who serve most fruitfully on the ministry teams of your congregation will be serving:
> * For the sake of the mission of Jesus Christ in your place and time,
> * Out of the sense of giftedness and calling that they discern through the support and encouragement of the congregation,
> * For whatever duration of time and in whatever capacity is suited to their circumstances and development as a disciple,
> * For as long as they breathe.

Let Go of Permanence

In congregations where leadership and organization are shaped around disciples like these, ministry teams will constantly be arising, evolving, reforming, and dissolving. Everyone will need to struggle a little bit to accept this reality.

God is eternal. Nothing else is. Disciples are called to put their entire trust in God, but there is something in human nature that wants a firm grasp on eternity. We want to trust in God, but we keep trying to build things that we foolishly believe will last forever. Pharaoh's build pyramids. Potentates build kingdoms and dynasties. Patriots build nations. Patriarchs build families.

Many of us ordinary church people build programs. We want them to last forever, or at least until we aren't around to watch them die. We believe that big, durable, and popular will assure permanence.

It might be a good idea to remember that the center of Christian faith and identity is a guy who was marginalized, vulnerable, unpopular with many, and only served one three-year term. Yet, the name of Jesus is more widely known and loved than that of any other in human history.

In 1982 I was pastor of a little country church with about forty or fifty people struggling quietly to be the presence of the good news in their community. Everyone there, me included, was talking about the Crystal Cathedral and Pastor Robert Schuller. "Why don't we Methodists do church as well as he does? When are we going to recover our influence? If they can do it, why can't we? What's the matter with us?"

In 2012 (that's 30 years, the rough span of my little ministry) The Crystal Cathedral went bankrupt. That little country church is still there with about forty or fifty people struggling quietly to be the presence of the good news to the people in their community. One could argue that this proves that a little, faithful country church is more valuable than a massive slick thing of a ministry with its own television station. I'm not sure that's the right lesson, though.

Durability isn't any better a measure than size when we're talking about Christian communities. The Crystal Cathedral may have lasted only forty years, but...
One of the elder women in that little open country church once confided in me, "You know, pastor, my daughter made some bad choices when she was young, and she ended up being a single mom with little babies living on her own in California. If it wasn't for the free daycare program and the

spiritual support and friendship they gave her at the Crystal Cathedral, I don't know if she ever would have gotten her life straightened out."

> *God is eternal. Nothing else is. Disciples are called to put their entire trust in God, but there is something in human nature that wants a firm grasp on eternity. We want to trust in God, but we keep trying to build things that we foolishly believe will last forever.*

The real measure of a disciple, of a ministry, or of a congregation, is impact. It is bringing others into the presence of the blessing of God. Eventually everything passes away. Disciples pass away; we call them saints.

Programs pass away. Churches pass away. Even denominations pass away. The value of them all is not their durability, neither is it their size. It is the impact they have while they are here. Our work as leaders is not to *preserve* these things, but to *spend* them on the impact they have in their place and time.

We will be blessed if we can trust the future to the Lord God of eternity instead of to the permanence of our institutions and programs.

My prayer is that this book might help you and your church find the root of its life in Jesus Christ and the mission that Christ has entrusted to you here and now. I hope it might help you learn to better work together as the Body of Christ to fulfill that mission. And I believe that in this, the life of faithful discipleship together, you will find the joy in living that Jesus called "shaken, patted down and overflowing."

Appendix A

A Process for Adopting Simple Governance (United Methodists)

1. **District Superintendent Consultation:** The pastor and/ or lay leader will contact the DS to inform them of the congregation's interest in adopting a simple governance model governance structure.

2. **Leadership Study:** The pastor and a core group of leaders from the congregation participate in a Simple Governance Workshop offered by the Conference.

3. **Council Action:** The church's administrative board or church council adopt a resolution requesting that the congregation move to a specific simple governance model that meets the Conference minimum standards.

4. **Town Hall:** The congregational leaders hold at least one town hall meeting of the congregation to present the new structure and the reasons for adopting it. The leaders will receive affirmations and concerns about the new structure, but no vote will be taken.

5. **Perfection:** Congregational leadership may amend the proposed structure to address concerns if that seems advisable. Another town hall meeting may be held if revisions are required.

6. **All-Church Conference:** Following approval of the proposed structure by the District Superintendent, she or he will call an All-Church Conference to consider the adoption of the new structure. No amendments will be allowed at this meeting. The congregation may debate the proposal, but it must vote up or down on the proposal as presented by church leadership.

Appendix B
Oregon-Idaho Simple Governance Model

The Parts:

Church Council:

The Council consists of twelve elected officers including the following disciplinary offices: the Lay Leader / Council Chair, and the Lay Members of Annual Conference. The Lead Pastor also serves on this council, so the total is 13 voting members.

1   Lay Leader / Church Council Chair

1   Lead Pastor

3   Members with facilities focus (3-year terms, each in one class)

3   Members with finance focus (3-year terms, each in one class)

3   Members with personnel focus (3-year terms, each in one class)

1   Lay Member of Annual Conference (¶252.5g "a lay member")

1   Other person (past Lay Leader? Lay Leader elect?)

?   Other positions as needed for your context

The Church Council is responsible (and has authority) to keep the entire ministry of the congregation focused on the mission. It sets the basic boundaries (policies) within which the congregation lives out its vision. Boundaries include allocation of resources (budget, paid staff positions), and ethical standards and adequate processes (such as financial practices and audits). It establishes goals for the overall effectiveness of the congregation in fulfilling its mission. It holds the Lead

Pastor accountable to fruitfulness in meeting the missional goals set for the congregation.

IMPORTANT – the entire council functions **together** as Trustees, Finance and SPRC. The people specifically elected in those areas of focus provide expertise, focus and information in their area of specialty, but do not make decisions apart from the council as a whole.

The Church Council is accountable to the mission (it is God's Church), to the standards of conduct for its members (such as participation in meetings, worship, giving and so on) and to the congregation (through their annual election of leaders to whom they entrust the mission of the congregation).

Committee on Nominations and Leadership Development:

The Discipline requires that there be a Committee on Nominations and Leadership Development (¶258.1). The committee is to be composed of not more than 9 persons elected to 3-year terms in 3 classes, plus the lay leader and pastor. The pastor shall be the chair of this committee.

This committee will work with the pastor throughout the year to identify, call and equip leadership for the mission of the congregation. They shall annually recommend to the Charge Conference a slate of qualified and called persons for election to all elected offices in the congregation. When elected offices become vacant for any reason in between charge conferences the committee will make nominations to the Church Council for ad-interim election to fill these vacancies.

Ministry Teams:

There may be as many ministry teams as there are ministries. A ministry may be a regular, ongoing program (such as a weekly worship service or the youth fellowship group), an annual event (like as a volunteer recognition dinner or family retreat), or even a single major event (a one-time mission trip).

Every ministry will have a ministry team. Ministry teams may be almost any size, depending on the demands of the ministry they are carrying out and each ministry team will have a ministry team leader.

Every ministry team leader is a staff person, whether paid or unpaid. Staff persons are people who lead a ministry. The ministry team leader is responsible for organizing the people who are doing the specific ministry and for focusing the ministry team on the goals and outcomes that define its responsibility. The ministry team leaders (staff) all work within the alignment authority of the Lead Pastor who holds all the ministries accountable to the missional goals established by the Church Council.

Decisions about how (within the boundaries and policies) to reach the goals of a ministry will be made by the ministry team doing the ministry. The goals and methods of the ministry team will be established in consultation with the Lead Pastor in order to assure their alignment with the overarching ministry goals set by the Council. The ministry team leader will be accountable to see that the team is working toward fulfillment of those goals.

The Lead Pastor will establish adequate processes to ensure alignment of the ministry teams so that:

- each ministry understands and embraces its part in the overall mission of the congregation,

- ministries are not unnecessarily competing with or limiting one another,

- gaps in ministry are addressed, and

- mutual support and synergy are built between all the ministries of the congregation.

The primary authority of the Lead Pastor regarding ministry teams is to ensure alignment and fruitfulness. The responsibility of the Lead Pastor is equipping (inspiring), and deploying them toward fruitfulness in the mission, vision and values of the congregation as established by the Church Council.

ADDITIONAL OPTIONAL STRUCTURES

Some congregations may find it useful to utilize additional groupings of leaders to effectively fulfill their mission. Some such useful groupings are included here:

Church Council Executive Committee

A Church Council Executive Committee may be designated including the Council Chair/Lay Leader, the Pastor and one or two other members of the Church Council. This group would work between the quarterly meetings of the Council to prepare agenda, remind members of preparation assignments, consult with the pastoral leader about important decisions between meetings, and make decisions to call special meetings.

Mission and Ministry Core Team

Congregations may have a Mission and Ministry Core Team. The pastor and lay leader will lead this group. It will include all leaders elected by other church groups (such as United Methodist Women's President or representative, United Methodist Men's President or representative, or Youth Council President). It will also include the ministry team leaders (as identified by the pastor) of any other significant on-going program bodies in the church. This group will meet regularly as needed to coordinate ministry programs so that they are mutually supportive and well aligned with the mission of the congregation as a whole.

Appendix C
Annual Church Council Agenda

The simple governance model works best when the Church Council meets less often (quarterly) and in greater depth with a different agenda focus for each meeting. The model offered here assumes four Council meetings each year. Each session would be a semi-retreat setting of at least 4 hours in duration (well-prepared boards will prefer 6 hours) with the council sharing a meal. There are, however, a variety of ways to organize the work of the Church Council to accomplish its purpose. This is offered as an example and congregations are encouraged to adapt the process to support their mission and vision.

Meeting One - Looking Up: Orientation of new officers to the mission, vision, values and process of the Church Council. The council members will be led in a process of understanding and making commitment to the mission, vision and values of the congregation. There will learning about the role of each person on the board and how they work together for the benefit of the mission. The session should include some relationship and team building. This meeting may also include review of the boundaries/policies to make sure they are up to date and relevant to the mission.

Meeting Two - Looking Back: Evaluation of past year. This session will occur at a time when past-year information is available (statistics, finances, year-end reports, etc.) The council will compare the performance of the congregation to the goals established for that period. After an honest assessment of "how did we do in accomplishing what we set as goals?" the group will process the following questions: What in the past year should be celebrated in the congregation? Where we fell short, what were the reasons? What can we learn from our experience that will help us be more fruitful moving forward? Were our goals useful, and if not, what would have been more important for us to focus on? This meeting may include the group portion of pastoral evaluation.

Meeting Three - Looking Around: Grounding us in our current reality. This session will focus on the following questions (each member having prepared!): What are the strengths in our congregation right now? What are the challenges to our congregation right now? What new forces are emerging in our congregation that we should be attending to? What is happening in our community (mission field) that may have an impact on the congregation, or that call the congregation to have an impact in the community? Each person on the council will be bringing information about which they have specific knowledge (for example; facilities folks should report on the facilities - are they adequate, what major issues are present, what opportunities are presenting themselves? Personnel focus people would speak to staff and leadership matters. Finance focus people to finances, others to spiritual and program matters.)

Meeting Four - Looking Forward: Setting goals and measures for the coming year. This session will take the knowledge base generated in the previous two sessions and use it to set from one to four major goals for the coming year (with up to 3 years "in mind"). What missional outcomes do we feel God is calling us to achieve? What reallocation of resources might be required to achieve those outcomes? What do we need to stop doing in order to do what is needed now?

Meeting Five – All Church Meeting: The Council reports to the congregation the "state of the church and community." The council introduces the goals they have established for the coming year and explains how the resource plans (budget and staffing plan) is intended to help the congregation fulfill its goals. The congregation votes on the slate of officers being elected to lead the congregation in fulfilling the ministry they share.

Detailed Five-Meeting Agenda

Simple Governance, when done well, is a powerful way to focus the congregation in its mission and vision. However, most experienced congregational leaders have very little experience in governance and deeply ingrained habits to focus on management of programs. The following plan for four Church Council Meetings and one All-Church Meeting each year can help governing boards to attend to those matters they are called to care for, and to delegate management to the staff.

FIRST MEETING: LOOKING UP

This meeting will be the first meeting of the newly elected church council / governing board. In most congregations this will occur in January, but it can be any time of the year when new elected officers are coming on board. The other three meetings of the council / board must be in order relative to one another, but this one can fit in whenever new officers are installed.

Relationship Grounding ....20 min
Introductions and relationship building exercise
Bible Study on Discipleship or Mission (pastor) ....40 min
Review of Mission / Vision / Core Values (Chair) ....90 min
* What are they? How and when were they developed?
* What do they mean to us personally?
* How do we define a "disciple" in our congregation?
* How are we as leaders expected to model and manifest the mission/vision?
* Do they still represent the core convictions of our congregation about the will of God for us here and now? (Is it time to "revise" them?)
Lunch (or dinner) ....45 min
Our Role as Council / Board (Chair) ....60 min
* What are the expectations of us on the council / board?
* Time commitment to our work (meetings and between meetings)
* Specific Board-member job descriptions (for example who is especially responsible for attention to finance, personnel, facilities, etc.?)
* Confidentiality – transparency / communication
Reflection / Sending (pastor)...45 min
* Opportunities for participants to reflect together on the ministry of the council / board.

218

- Evaluation of the day – What was helpful / useful / inspiring? What was discouraging / wasted time / frustrating?
- Devotional sending

SECOND MEETING: LOOKING BACK

The purpose of this meeting is an honest evaluation of the previous year in ministry. It should mostly be centered on one to four specific goals that were established in the "Looking Forward" meeting about a year and a half previous. The meeting will occur at a time when data on the goals can be gathered and presented to the council. No new goals are developed at this meeting! The atmosphere is "What can we learn from what actually happened when we did what we did?"

Relationship Grounding ....20 min
- Introductions and relationship building exercise

Bible Study around Evaluation/Review (pastor) ....40 min

Review of Past Year Data (chair & others)......................45 min
- Finances (fund raising, spending, surprises?)
- Attendance / membership / or other participation measures

Review Past Year Goals (chair & others).........................45 min
- Begin working through the goals set for the past year. Look at each one in turn with the following questions in mind:
- Did we achieve the goal we set? To what degree?
- If yes,
  - Did it move us forward in our mission and vision?
  - Did it help us make disciples of Jesus Christ for the transformation of the world?
  - Could we have done even better and if so how?
  - What unexpected outcomes (+/-) came as a result of this effort?
- If no,
  - Was it because we didn't do what we intended?

- Was it unrealistic or did we fail to do what we could have done?
- Did we do what we planned, but it just didn't work?
- What might we have done differently to achieve what we intended?
- What unexpected outcomes (+/-) came as a result of this effort?

Lunch (or dinner) ....45 min

Continue working through the previous year's goals .120 minutes

Reflection / Sending (pastor)..45 min
- Opportunities for participants to reflect together on the ministry of the council / board.
- Evaluation of the day – What was helpful / useful / inspiring? What was discouraging / wasted time / frustrating?
- Devotional sending

THIRD MEETING: LOOKING AROUND

This meeting is about getting our heads and hearts around the current reality in the church and the mission field in which we are doing ministry. It is not evaluative in the sense of judging good or bad. It is intended to be descriptive. Members of the council / board should each come to this meeting having prepared to share in particular areas of the agenda. Other persons in the church or community may also be invited to make presentations on specific areas that may be helpful to the council / board as it seeks to deeply understand its context.

Relationship Grounding ....20 min
- Introductions and relationship building exercise

Bible Study around Discipleship on context (pastor).........40 min
- Jesus and the prophets give us many examples of what it means to really see what is happening.

What is the "state of the church?" (Chair and others).......90 min

- Presentations and discussion around the following topics
- What is the current state of our facilities with respect to our mission?
- What is the current state of our staff with attention to their morale, skills, commitment, compensation, and the overall makeup of the staff team?
- What is the current state of our finances?
- What is our current program profile– what is actually being done by in and through the church?
- What is working? What is not working?
- Are their "gaps" in any of these areas?

Lunch (or dinner) ....45 min

What is the state of the mission field? (Chair and others) .60 min

- What is our mission field? (City, county, particular population, etc.?)
- What is happening in our mission field? (economic issues, major tragedies or new developments, political changes, natural disasters, new or lost major institutions such as schools, colleges, hospitals, employers?)
- This time may be guided discussion, reports by interested council / board members, or even a guest speaker to share about a specific community issue.
- Open discussion, "What aspects of our mission field may have an impact on what God wants from our church in this context?" No program planning should occur! Just an open discussion of what might matter to God in this reality.

Reflection / Sending (pastor)..45 min

- Opportunities for participants to reflect together on the ministry of the council / board.
- Evaluation of the day – What was helpful / useful / inspiring? What was discouraging / wasted time / frustrating?
- Devotional sending

FOURTH MEETING: LOOKING AHEAD

At this meeting the council / board will establish three to five focus goals that will direct the attention of the congregation for the coming year. They will be informed by the current goals in place (established at the previous Looking Ahead meeting, and currently being carried out by the congregation). These goals should be clear and will serve as the major accountability guide for the pastor and staff.

Relationship Grounding ....20 min
  * Introductions and relationship building exercise

Bible Study on intentional mission (pastor).....................40 min
  * (In the Book of Acts, almost every story begins with the implementation of a plan intended to accomplish the mission. While these plans rarely go as intended, they generate the movement that gets redirected through all the accidents and contingencies toward the intention of God.)

Where is God calling us 3 – 5 years out? (Chair) ....90 min
  * Guided discussion around the following questions:
  * Who are we called to reach that we are not connecting with now? How might God be broadening our mission field?
  * What current strengths afford us opportunities to deepen and expand our faithfulness and fruitfulness?
  * What challenges in our church are calling for us to give special attention to strengthening or improving current ministries?
  * Which of these callings, opportunities or challenges seem to offer the greatest promise of increasing our fruitfulness if we can address them?
  * Which of these are beyond our capability at this time?
  * Narrow the list of possibilities to one to four worthy of special focus.

Lunch (or dinner) ....45 min
Strategic Plans ....100 min

- What current ministries or programs have a role to play in these focus areas?
- What specific outcomes would we plan to see in each of these focus areas? (These will be specific, measurable outcomes the would represent success in addressing the calling.)
- Who will be delegated authority to develop specific ministry plans to address each of these focus areas? What authorities to they need (finances, people, facilities) in order to have an opportunity to accomplish the outcomes?
- What new ministries or programs might be required in order to adequately address these focus areas?
- What current ministries or programs might need to be curtailed or diminish in emphasis in order to accomplish these outcomes?

Assignments ....20 min
- Who is the person responsible for each focus area getting to the next step?

Reflection / Sending (pastor)..45 min
- Opportunities for participants to reflect together on the ministry of the council / board.
- Evaluation of the day – What was helpful? What was frustrating?
- Devotional sending

FIFTH MEETING: ALL-CHURCH MEETING

At this meeting all members and friends of the church are welcome to attend and to participate. It is Chaired by the chair of the church council / board. All the members of the church council / board will be present if at all possible and play a role in leading – this meeting "belongs" to the council / board.

The meeting should incorporate elements of prayer and singing at various points throughout).

Devotional on Discipleship or Mission (pastor)................15 min
Review of Mission / Vision / Core Values (Chair)...........30 min
- What are they? How and when were they developed?
- What do they mean to us personally?
- How do we define a "disciple" in our congregation?

Share the state of the church ....30 min
- How and what did we do in the previous year – finances, programs, facilities staff?
- What are our strengths and challenges?
- What were our specific focus goals, how did we do at attaining them, and what did we learn?

What goals are we proposing for the coming year? ....30 min
- Go through them one at a time. What, Why, Who, When?

What is our resource plan for the coming year? ....15 min
- Budget
- Staffing plan (paid and unpaid)
- Facilities (any changes in use or major remodeling or building plans?)

Election of Leaders (Lay Leader) ....30 min
- The process used by the Committee on Nominations and Lay Leadership in calling leaders and the qualifications they seek in leaders, are explained.
- The leaders continuing in office are introduced.
- Nominations list for new leaders is presented and the nominees are introduced.
- The congregation votes on the slate of elected leaders presented by the Committee on Nominations and Lay Leadership.

Closing Devotion (Pastor) ....15 min
- Dedication of both leaders and the congregation to fulfillment of the calling their share in mission to their community and the world.

Charge Conference

United Methodists will also have an annual Charge Conference according to the Disciplinary requirements for that meeting. It will come after the All-Church meeting. All the necessary reports and decision that belong to the charge conference will be made by the charge conference. There should not be votes on those issues at the All-Church meeting. The exception is the election of officers. In that case the Charge Conference will ratify the slate of officers elected at the All-Church meeting.

Special Council Meetings

Special Meetings: There can always arise emergency situations that overcome normal protocol and boundaries. The sewer mainline collapses and an $8000 repair is required that doesn't fit in the facilities budget. The facilities manager is uncomfortable making a. "executive decision" of such moment, and the pastor isn't quite happy just saying, "Go ahead," either. At times like this a special church council meeting is called very quickly and the council considers the specific issue and provides a process for resolving the question.

Appendix D
Town Hall Meetings

Town Hall Meetings: The council may hold town hall meetings anytime they deem a significant issue to be worthy of consideration and input by the whole congregation. Generally there would be no more than two or three of these in a given year. These meetings will be holy conferencing. Any particular town hall meeting will be for the purpose of receiving input on just one question. (Shall we expand our facilities? Should we add a new campus? Will we undertake sponsoring a daughter congregation? Should we add an additional weekly worship experience?) There are no votes at town hall meetings. All council members are to be present to hear the input.

Process:

This is not a debate. It is holy conferencing. The purpose of holy conferencing is to assist the body in listening to one another and to the Holy Spirit in our midst so that we can discern God's will for us on this particular issue. It is not an opportunity for each of us to try to change everyone else's mind, nor to engage in discussion about other matters.

Make it clear that the Board or Council is presenting background information and either its best idea of a way forward, or a series of possible options. A final plan is NOT yet in place, and the Town Hall meeting is for the purpose of gathering information and feedback in order to develop a plan that represents the congregation's wisdom and that can earn its support.   .

The matters we are considering involve matters of great significance in the life of our church. Many of us may experience strong feelings such as fear, anxiety, hope, expectation, confusion, grief, and gratitude. We will strive to respect and honor one another in the midst of this tumult of feeling. The general process practiced at a town hall meeting is:

a) The Board/Council will present its background information on the issue and best ideas for moving forward.

b) Each person present will have an opportunity to state his or her own responses.

c) No on has the authority to speak for anyone else, especially anonymous "others."

d) No one will be afforded an opportunity to speak twice until everyone has had a chance to speak once on each question.

e) In order to honor the time available, all will strive to consider their statements to keep them clear, focused and brief.

f) Everyone will address all those gathered and avoid speaking in opposition or correction of another's statement.

g) Questions will be answered as accurately and clearly as possible by persons in a position to know the answer. If none present have an answer it will be obtained (if possible) and made available. Some (many!) questions have no answers.

Sample Agenda 1:

1. Opening Prayer
2. Introduction of Process
3. Board / Council presents the issue for consideration and any background information they have developed.
4. Board / Council presents any initial idea or ideas they have developed regarding the way forward. (This step may be skipped if there is no plan or options yet prepared, though it is usually best to present some ideas!)
5. Everyone has an opportunity to respond to the following questions in turn.
   a. What question do you have about the board / council's presentation?
   b. What do you most value in the board / council's presentation?
   c. What concern do you have of any of the board / council's report?
   d. What additional information or suggestions do you have regarding this issue?
6. Closing Prayer

Sample Agenda 2:

1. Opening Prayer
2. Introduction of Process
3. Introduce the issue or challenge being addressed.
4. Share one of the proposed alternatives for moving forward.
   a. What one thing do you appreciate in this alternative?

    b.   What is your greatest concern regarding this alternative?

    c.   What question do you have regarding this alternative?

5.   Repeat for all the alternative solutions that have been explored.

6.   Closing Prayer

Annotated Bibliography on Governance

Winning on Purpose: How To Organize Congregations to Succeed in Their Mission, by John Edmund Kaiser, Abingdon Press 2006.

All the ideas around the alignment of responsibility, authority and accountability come from this book. The strength of this book is its straightforward and uncompromising approach to congregational governance. Written from a free-church tradition, it does not translate very easily for congregations in connectional polities (United Methodists, Presbyterians, Lutherans and others). It is also very pastor-centered in a way that would put some congregations (and even some pastors!) in open rebellion. The book relies heavily on sports metaphors, which some find very useful and others confusing or even off-putting.

Governance and Ministry: Rethinking Board Leadership, by Dan Hotchkiss, The Alban Institute 2009.

The ideas about the value of flat and simple organizations come substantially from this book. Dan Hotchkiss is perhaps the most insightful contemporary author on issues around non-profit governance. The book covers all the theory and practice of effective governance systems extremely well. For anyone looking for a deeper background in the principles of governance, this is the book. Precisely because it is thorough and complete it is a bit academic for some readers and is often thin on recognizable examples to make the material accessible for volunteer church leaders.

I Refuse to Lead a Dying Church, by Paul Nixon, Pilgrim Press, 2006.

The significance of a renewed and compelling focus on mission, vision and values come from this book. Paul does a great job of conveying the character and source of the malaise that afflicts many American congregations. He is compelling in his passion to be part of the revitalization of our faith communities. He also hits all the right buttons about what kind of leadership it takes for congregations to find new life in the midst of the challenges they face.

Canoeing the Mountains: Christian Leadership in Uncharted Territory, by Tod Bolsinger, IVP, 2015.

Using the story of the Lewis and Clarke expedition as a model, Tod explores the qualities required to lead in circumstances where the context is unanticipated and poorly understood. He makes the case that our current challenge as church leaders is that we are in an unanticipated and poorly understood context and lays out some of the lessons we may take from Lewis and Clarke.

The Anatomy of Peace, by The Arbinger Institute, The Arbinger Institute, 2015

Exploring the mindset and practices that lead to peaceful, just and enduring resolution of conflict. The practices shared here apply in both individual and community situations like those frequently occurring in congregations.

Made in the USA
Columbia, SC
06 November 2024

45824196R00128